OUT OF BOUNDS

*G*irls wading off Fisherman's Island, Toronto, circa 1907.

OUT OF BOUNDS

Women, Sport and Sexuality

by Helen Lenskyj

Dedicated to my children, Lisa and Nicolas.

PHOTO CREDITS

Action Sport Photography Toronto: p. 108
Joan Blackwood: p.103.
Jerry Cohen and Norman Cohen: p.134.
Doris Craig, personal collection: p.54.
Foote Collection, Manitoba Archives: pp.22, 42, 43.
James Collection, City of Toronto Archives: pp. 4, 21, 31, 34, 37, 65.
Liz Martin: p.126.
Ontario Archives: p.67.
Toronto Board of Education Archives: Cover, pp.72, 91, 94, 100.
Judy McClara: p.116.

CANADIAN CATALOGUING IN PUBLICATION DATA
Lenskyj, Helen
Out of bounds: women, sport & sexuality

ISBN 0-88961-105-X

1. Sports for women — History. 2. Femininity (Psychology).
3. Sex — Social aspects. I. Title.

GV709.L45 1986   796'.01'94   C86-094711-4

Cover photo: Track and field meet, Toronto Board of Education, undated.
This book was produced by the collective effort
of the members of the Women's Press
Printed and bound in Canada.

Published by the Women's Press
517 College Street, suite 233
Toronto, Ontario M6G 4A2

CONTENTS

ACKNOWLEDGEMENTS

I WOULD LIKE to thank my feminist friends and colleagues, especially those at the Ontario Institute for Studies in Education, for their help and support in the writing of this book. I also wish to acknowledge the financial assistance that I received from the Ontario Arts Council. Finally, I want to thank the women at Women's Press for invaluable editing assistance.

INTRODUCTION

THIS IS A HISTORY of women and sport during the past century. Although dramatic in many respects, developments during this period were not always progressive for women. As in other areas of women's lives, progress was frequently followed by periods of retrenchment. Sporting ability was hardly compatible with women's traditional subordinate role in patriarchal society; in fact, sport had the potential to equalize relations between the sexes. By minimizing socially constructed sex differences that had only tenuous biological bases, sport posed a serious threat to the myth of female frailty.

In the face of male opposition to their full sporting participation, some women accepted the restricted activities permitted by the "experts" — but just as many resisted male control. Their resistance prompted reaction on both a cultural and a structural level. The mass media portrayed women's athletic competence — beyond the requirements of general and reproductive health — as unfeminine and unattractive to men, while, within the sport system formal rules and restrictions, justified as "protection," excluded girls and women from the full range of physical activities.

By the turn of the century, community organizations were offering sport and recreational programs for the growing numbers of young working-class men and women whose uncontrolled leisure was seen as a potential social problem. Schools and universities were also expanding their athletic programs, but the alleged threat to femininity posed by sport had the effect of limiting female participation to the least demanding, most feminine of activities. Social class played an important part in determining which girls and women would have access to these institutions. Since education past the age of compulsory attendance was not considered essential for young women whose sole destiny was domesticity and motherhood, it was a low priority in families with limited financial resources.

As industry became more mechanized, sex differences in strength became increasingly irrelevant to occupational patterns; during the war years, for example, women filled jobs in the munitions industry which had formerly been held by men. These trends had important implications for sport. When traditional sex differentiation in the workplace was no longer tenable, male physical dominance acted out on the playing field gained greater symbolic importance. Sex differences were reinforced and entrenched by excluding women from the "manly" sports and thus legitimizing, once again, the notion that male physical superiority and male supremacy were inextricably linked. Despite the restrictions, however, the hundred-year period from the 1880s to the present marked women's entry into almost every avenue of sport.

♦   ♦   ♦

The connections between female sexuality and feminist analysis are convincingly articulated by Catherine MacKinnon. She argues that the relationship between sexuality and feminism parallels that between work and Marxism; in both instances, control is the central issue. Abuses of women are abuses of sex, manifestations of "male pursuit of control over female sexuality."[1] A major component of female sexuality is the female reproductive function.

The processes by which powerful alliances of men exercise control over female sexuality are central to the analysis. The dominant group — white upper-class males — achieves consensus on the cultural and ideological dimensions of female sexuality through the ideas of male "experts" in medicine, science and religion. Thus, class, race and gender inequality — unequal economic, social and political relations between the dominant and subordinate group — is maintained. These ends are achieved, not by force, but by consensus, so that "common sense," like Marx's "false consciousness," is no longer "good sense," despite its deceptive aura of naturalness or sanctity. Women are therefore unlikely to develop a complete and accurate consciousness of the nature of their oppression.[2] However, women should not be portrayed simply as victims in a male-dominated society that systematically discriminates against them. Many women were shaping, as well as being shaped, by the attitudes and practices surrounding femininity, female sexuality and female reproductive function.

In all areas of female sexuality — from reproductive rights to sexual expression — male control has traditionally been present in the guise of moral and biological rationales: doctors, scientists and clergymen were the experts. More recently, psychologists and psychiatrists have been exercising power on questions of female sexuality, while at the same time depoliticizing the issues by defining them as private, personal matters.

Of particular relevance to the study of women and sport is the "political institution" of compulsory heterosexuality.[3] In their attempts to explain why some girls and women enjoyed and even excelled at "masculine" sports, experts proposed that either participation made them masculine or that they were masculine at the outset. Although connotations of terms such as "masculine," "mannish" and "tomboy" changed during the century, the stigma remained. The "tomboys" and the women who "played like men" defied the bounds of femininity and heterosexuality.

The traditional feminine attributes of passivity, dependence and nurturance are an essential part of the patriarchal view of the woman as the submissive, subordinate partner in male/female relationships. Femininity is therefore more than simply an aesthetic; it is the concrete manifestation of women's subordinate status. Consequently, activities that are incompatible with this image of women are, not surprisingly, seen as a threat to existing power relations between the sexes which are predicated, at the most basic level, on male strength and female weakness.

The links between ideology, female sexuality and sporting participation become clear when we examine what exactly constitutes female sexuality in this context. It encompasses the anatomical and physiological, and the social and expressive, as well as the interaction of the two; it relates to all aspects of the female reproductive function, sexual expression and presentation of self as female.

The relationship between sport, femininity and sexuality will be investigated in the first two chapters by analysing the issue of medical control over the female reproductive function, as seen in medical restrictions on girls' and women's sporting participation. The remaining chapters will deal with broader questions of male control as female sexuality became differentiated from the female reproductive function and as the evolving concept of heterosexuality further legitimized constraints on women in sport.

It is hoped that by understanding women's sporting heritage and by becoming alert to the ways in which sport has been, and continues to be, coopted for the purpose of male control over female sexuality and the female reproductive function, women will be strengthened in the struggle for autonomy in sport.

♦

Woman working with exercise apparatus,
from William Anderson, Anderson's Physical Education
(Toronto: Harold Wilson, n.d.), p.30.

CHAPTER ONE

DOCTORS HAVE
THE FIRST WORD

OVER THE PAST CENTURY, the medical profession has played a dominant role in dictating safe and appropriate sporting activities for women. This dominance may be understood as yet another instance of medical control over women's lives in general, and over reproduction in particular.[1]

By the late 1800s, doctors were expanding their professional influence and their moral leadership on questions of women's health and women's place in society. Public health movements, through school and community programs, were bringing mothers, infants and school children under medical influence. Medical advice literature — books, pamphlets, magazine articles — was becoming increasingly accessible to women of all social classes. Health professionals were addressing female health issues at meetings and conferences on education, recreation, social service and social reform. Male doctors were directing athletic programs in a significant number of colleges and universities throughout Canada and the U.S.A.

At the turn of the century, when female sporting participation had become sufficiently widespread to attract public and medical attention, gynecology was well established as a specialized and profitable field in North America. The revival of the modern Olympics in 1896 and the formalization of school and university athletic programs at this time sparked early medical interest in the physiological aspects of sport. This resulted in the subsequent specialization of sportsmedicine, a field which had its official beginnings in the 1920s.

As women challenged traditional constraints on education, work and leisure pursuits in the last half of the nineteenth century, doctors reacted with efforts to establish women's physical and intellectual inferiority. They cited sex differences ranging from smaller brains to lighter bones to support their claims. Doctors also adhered to the widely held Victorian principle that women were the morally superior gender, the natural models of sexual and moral virtue, and therefore all the more blameworthy when they fell from grace. To jeopardize their god-given capacity to bear children, by straining body or brain, defied both common sense and divine decree.

The two themes converged in doctors' consideration of female sporting participation. Both women's unique anatomy and physiology and their special moral obligations disqualified them from vigorous physical activity. Women had a moral duty to preserve their vital energy for childbearing and to cultivate personality traits suited to the wife-and-mother role. Sport wasted vital force, strained female bodies and fostered traits unbecoming to "true womanhood."

The medical profession's power and influence in these matters extended to women of all backgrounds, although medical priorities reflected class and ethnic biases. Doctors viewed the reproductive capacity of Anglo-Saxon, middle-class women as a more valuable commodity than that of their working-class, immigrant counterparts. They monitored the reproductive health of young women in private schools and universities more carefully than that of women who left school early for factory work or domestic service. Nevertheless, the myths surrounding menstruation — particularly prohibitions against swimming, bathing and strenuous activity during the period — were widely held, even though many women defied these restrictions.

More leisure hours and a greater range of organized sport and physical activities were available to privileged women, while time, energy and financial resources were scarce for most working-class women at the end of their long work days. Marriage and motherhood reduced recreational opportunities for women of all classes; those who could afford domestic help had some leisure time, but it was more acceptable for middle-class wives and mothers to do charity work than to play tennis.

The bicycle, introduced in the late 1800s, significantly increased the leisure options for all women. Even working-class women could afford the relatively cheap rental or purchase price of a bicycle. In the face of a cycling craze that involved mass female participation throughout North America, doctors and other custodians of female morality eventually abandoned their crusade against the attire and activities of the "lady cyclist." Thus, cycling played an important part in liberating nineteenth-century women from rigid Victorian standards of acceptable dress and appropriate public behaviour.

MODESTY IS A VIRTUE

Medical control of women's health and by extension their lifestyles and leisure activities was facilitated by the popularity of vitalist theories of physiology. Vitalism held that energy for the human organism was derived from a "vital force," which, being limited and non-renewable, should therefore be expended only in the service of family, god or country. Although references to vitalism had become relatively rare in medical literature by the 1900s, terms such as "vital energy" and "nervous force" had entered popular usage, and appeared in non-medical literature well into the twentieth century. As late as 1935, an article on the dangers of girls' basketball in the American Medical Association publication *Hygeia* presented a classic nineteenth-century vitalist explanation:

> In some cases, basketball can make too heavy a demand on the organic vitality of a growing girl ... a great deal of the excess energy is needed for the physical changes which are naturally taking place.[2]

Vitalist theories effectively supported the female frailty myth. The development of the reproductive system in the pubescent girl and its subsequent complex functioning demanded the lion's share of her vital energy. Menarche (onset of first menstruation), the menstrual cycle, pregnancy, lactation and menopause were portrayed as the "waves of functional life" that every woman must weather.[3] Each event constituted a heavy drain on vital energy and left little surplus for physical activity or "brainwork." Women were therefore constitutionally frail. Conversely, if a woman's lifestyle was excessively strenuous, either physically, intellectually or emotionally, her reproductive function would suffer. Any drain on her vital force could result in retarded breast development or amenorrhea (temporary cessation of menstruation).[4]

One of the main functions of vitalist theories appears to have been the medical control of male sexual activities. Male masturbation and sexual excess were doctors' primary targets, probably because it was relatively easy to argue that "vital energy" (in the form of seminal fluid) was visibly drained by these activities. Female masturbation and sexual activities did not produce the same clear "evidence"; however, by the 1890s prescriptive literature directed at girls and women reflected doctors' growing awareness that masturbation was not an exclusively male pursuit. Women, too, wasted their vital force in this way. Gynecology texts described the symptoms of this harmful practice and the creative methods used by female masturbators of all ages lest any seemingly innocuous activity escape the doctor's notice. Medical literature frequently linked physical activity and female masturbation noting that, since the devil finds work for "idle hands," sport and exercise were effective therapy: "to replace is to conquer." An unforeseen complication, however, was the sexual pleasure allegedly derived from certain gymnastic exercises. Similar suspicions had been a factor in doctors' censure of female cyclists in the 1890s, but by 1913 at least one gynecologist admitted that the bicycle saddle should be exonerated.[5]

Both female sporting participation and masturbation allowed girls and women to become more attuned to, and familiar with, their bodies, but female masturbation had particularly serious implications. Medical control over female physicality and sexuality depended as much on women's moral sensibilities as on their ignorance of their physical and sexual potential. Modesty in

*M*iss Beaton's swimming class at McGill Street Y.W.C.A.,
Toronto, circa 1907.

dress, appearance and deportment reflected a woman's acceptance of both her pedestal and her prison.

Female modesty became a favourite topic among doctors in
the 1870s and 1880s when the bloomer was beginning to be worn
by increasing numbers of active women. Modesty, according to
these medical men, required clothing that concealed the limbs,
especially the legs, and ensured that the wearer could not move in
the free, vigorous manner associated with masculinity.[6] The
voluminous folds of the skirt necessitated slow, graceful
movement and hid the fact that "a woman really had more than
one leg."[7] Furthermore, modesty barred "good women" from
discussing or even naming the problematic areas that the skirt
concealed. As long as women's physical and sexual identities
remained cloaked in mystery and shame, women were poorly
equipped to question male medical authority.

Good women... possess no language and no terminology,
either for their feelings or their anatomy.

Dr. Howard Kelly, *Medical Gynecology*, 2nd ed.
(New York: D. Appleton, 1913), p. 314.

While most late nineteenth-century medical sources attributed a relatively weak sex drive to women, doctors believed that, once aroused, women's sexual energy could exceed the bounds of male intervention and control. Although school was identified as a "danger zone" where girls might be introduced to the masturbation habit, doctors displayed no particular apprehension regarding lesbian activity in schools. Their primary concerns were the alleged insatiability of the female sex drive and the possibility that "normal coitus" would not satisfy women who had discovered the pleasures of masturbation. However, one gynecologist acknowledged that male ignorance of female sexuality was a factor in women's dissatisfaction.[8] Condemnation of female masturbation reflected underlying fears that male dominance would be threatened by women's self-knowledge.

DUTY BEFORE PLEASURE

Women at Winnipeg Beach, circa 1913.

Medical classification of acceptable and unacceptable demands on vital force was shaped by the view that woman's destiny was to serve others. Higher education, employment, social engagements, and recreational pursuits were commonly identified as threats to female health. Athletics was believed to promote excessive muscular development, depleting "nerve-essence" and contributing to difficult childbirth and inferior offspring, but long hours devoted to housework and the care of parents, husband or children apparently involved no risk.[9] New York gynecologist Angenette Parry reported widespread medical censure of "women who live easy lives ... [with] not enough housework to take the place of athletics," and "patients worn out with social duties."[10]

Some doctors attempted to popularize housework as exercise, or as therapy for "young ladies" with health problems. According to one male expert, "All that is needed to make the delicate creatures well is to require them to change places with their mothers for a few weeks or months." "For ladies," he stated, "housework is admirably adapted to bring into play all the different muscles of the body."[11]

[She] could swing a six-pound dumb-bell,
    She could fence, and she could box,
She could row upon the river,
    She could clamber on the rocks.
She could do some heavy bowling,
    And play tennis all day long,
But she couldn't help her mother,
    As she wasn't very strong.

Dr. Elizabeth Mitchell,
"The Rise of Athleticism Among Women and Girls,"
National Council of Women of Canada Yearbook, 1895
(Montreal: John Lovell, 1896), p. 107.

An article on "Woman as an Athlete" by Dr. Arabella Kenealy typified medical responses to the "New Woman" whose appearance and lifestyle challenged existing definitions of femininity. The New Woman cycled and golfed when she should have been sewing for her sister, helping her brother with his homework, or soothing her father's "ruffled temper." The masculinizing effects of athletics also extended to the personality. Woman's natural sympathy was replaced by assertiveness, muscular achievement outpaced moral development, and the "dainty, elusive quality" of women's natural expression gave way to the "bicycle face," or "the face of muscular tension."[12] This feminine image of elusiveness or mystery which so often inspired male critics of the New Woman, was, of course, the privilege of class: middle-class men (and women) rarely agonized over the absence of daintiness, serenity and mystery on the sweating, straining faces of women who laboured in their kitchens, laundries and factories.

While medical critics condemned excessive female physical activity, they generally agreed that carefully regulated and supervised exercise was beneficial, both for general well-being and for female functional health. Physical training had become an established part of the program at several American women's colleges by the turn of the century, and studies demonstrated the positive effects of gymnastics and rowing on health and academic achievement.[13]

Doctors were slow to acknowledge the health and recreational benefits of cycling; some even suggested that pedalling a sewing machine afforded equivalent exercise. Apparently, it was reasonable to demand that women spend their leisure time "productively" (sewing) rather than "unproductively" (cycling), although no such rule was applied to men's leisure.[14] Yet some doctors were repudiating the "old Puritan idea" of duty, which condemned recreation as "pleasure for the sake of pleasure."[15]

There is no reason to think a healthy woman can be injured [cycling] ...*provided she does not over-exert herself by riding too long a time, or too fast, or up too steep hills, and provided she does not ride when common sense and physiology alike forbid any needless exertion.*

Dr. J. West Roosevelt,
"A Doctor's View of Bicycling,"
Scribner's (June 1895): 712

> Every year some new avenue, some new form of physical exercise is being opened to women. What was once frowned down upon as unladylike, trivial and shocking, is now done openly and with the approval of the beholders. Perhaps nothing illustrates this so much as the riding of the bicycle.
>
> Dr. Grace Ritchie, "Discussion,"
> *National Council of Women of Canada Yearbook, 1895*
> (Montreal: John Lovell, 1896), p. 117.

THE MONTHLY INCAPACITY

Increased female participation in sport by the end of the nineteenth century gave new prominence to the issue of medical restrictions on women's physical activity during menstruation. It needs to be understood in the wider context of women's reproductive health because menstruation was both a symbolic and a concrete reminder of fertility and femaleness. Moreover, its regular appearance reinforced the existing power relations between men and women: women experienced this monthly "incapacity," men did not.

At the turn of the century, malestream gynecology termed women's normal life changes "The Diseases of Women," and treated any menstrual variation as a condition demanding heroic medical intervention. In cases of amenorrhea, for example, poultices, mustard baths, leeches and vaginal injections were recommended to induce the period.[16] Many male doctors based their recommendations primarily on clinical practice; obviously, they saw more women who experienced menstruation-related health problems than women whose menstrual cycles were problem-free. At stake was the principle of male medical control over female sexuality, a problem that continues today in doctors' unequivocal pronouncements on the nature of the "normal" menstrual cycle.

Not surprisingly, it was women in the medical profession who redefined menstruation as a normal function rather than a sickness, and encouraged women to maintain a normal lifestyle regardless of the menstrual cycle. They documented the menstrual histories of large numbers of women over spans of several years in order to show that menstruation was not experienced as disabling by the majority of women.[17]

However, women's trustworthiness on matters of health, exercise and menstruation presented a problem to many male doctors. While advocating moderate exercise for improved functional health, one doctor condemned the young woman who is "loath to give up her *amusements* during menstruation." He also censured those who continue "*pleasurable* exercise, no matter how severe, and dance, wheel and skate regardless of the period." The doctor noted that "even *sports*, basketball, tennis ... are followed by some."[18] Another bluntly stated that menstrual incapacity was of "a fictional nature."[19]

Whatever the motive, the implications were serious. Either menstrual pain was imaginary, or women were so untrustworthy, so self-centred and frivolous that they continued pleasurable activities throughout the month but avoided unpleasant obligations on the excuse of menstruation. Yet, for a woman to fulfil her destiny as mother, she was expected to monitor all her activities in the light of possible danger to her reproductive function. Failure to do so constituted a failure to fulfil her religious, moral and patriotic duty: motherhood is "the most sacred trust the Almighty can bestow upon any woman."[20] The woman who ignored medical warnings regarding sporting participation challenged the primacy of the uterus.

Maternal obligations were, of course, affected by race and class. Mass immigration, wartime manpower losses and high birthrates in certain racial and ethnic groups fueled racist fears of Anglo-Saxon race suicide. Therefore there was a premium on the fertility of middle-class Anglo-Saxon women. In addition, working-class women were not expected to find menstruation, pregnancy or any other "diseases of women" as disabling as their more privileged counterparts.

Dr. Mary Jacobi's 1877 study, *The Question of Rest for Women During Menstruation*, concluded that, for women whose nutrition was adequate, rest was unnecessary, even undesirable, and that exercise was important to painless menstruation.[21] Some forty years later, Stanford professor Clelia Mosher demonstrated that the strengthening of the abdominal wall by means of a simple exercise served to ease menstrual pain. Her extensive research also showed that tight clothing, thoracic breathing and physical activity contributed to uterine congestion and menstrual pain.[22]

In the 1920s, findings that menstrual disorders affected only a minority of young women, and were responsive to simple treatment (warm baths), led some doctors to advise that all female students should participate regularly in games and exercise. Moreover, they noted that menstrual variations need not cause alarm; they were commonly associated with changes in surroundings and the social and mental strain of work or study.[23] A four-year study of college women found that the incidence of dysmenorrhea (painful menstruation) decreased as posture and muscle tone improved. The only treatment was the required college course in physical education and corrective posture exercises.[24]

WOMEN'S DELICATE ORGANS

Very little medical research investigated the alleged injury to the reproductive function through sporting participation until the 1920s, although lack of evidence did not weaken the medical position that caution should be the guiding principle in these matters. Many doctors linked athletics to complications of childbirth. They claimed that less flexible pelvic floor muscles prolonged labour and that "over-developed arms and legs" robbed the reproductive system of vital force.[25] An additional concern, unrelated to the usual vitalist arguments, was that physical activity caused uterine displacement, believed to be associated with dysmenorrhea and sterility.

In the 1800s, the causes most commonly cited in medical discussions of displacement were tight lacing and heavy clothing, "sexual excess," general debility, and strain and lacerations in childbirth.[26] By 1912, some gynecologists were claiming that "violent exercise," especially during menstruation, caused displacement, and were blaming athletics for exacerbating existing uterine problems.[27] It was believed that exercise during menstruation was dangerous because strain on the uterine ligaments was greatest when the uterus was heaviest. If this were true, however, the day before the period would be an equally dangerous time. The unpredictability of both the menstrual cycle and the female psyche defied total medical intervention or control, and it was probably this knowledge that led doctors eventually to forbid all strenuous activity.

The activity most commonly associated with displacement was jumping. One of the first lists classifying acceptable and unacceptable sports for girls, published in 1916, proscribed high jump, broad jump, competitive and men's rules basketball.[28] The same year, a prominent Canadian physical educator, Ethel Cartwright, included a similar list in an article on girls' athletics, advocating only "moderate physical exercise without jumps or strain" and forbidding competition during menstruation.[29]

As basketball became the focus of considerable controversy during the 1920s and 1930s, it is useful to compare the differences between "men's rules" and "girls' rules." Basketball began as a men's game in 1891; the next year, Senda Berenson, physical director at Smith College, had introduced the game with modified rules to her students. Her philosophy was typical of the period. She believed that sports, particularly a game like basketball, developed courage, self-denial, self-control and "gentle manners"— all desirable qualities of "true womanhood." Her modifications to the game were intended to control the "roughness" — the body contact and risk of falling — and to reduce its demands on speed and endurance.[30] The modified game restricted players' movement to specific sections of the court and allowed no interference between players. It moved "on the pace of ping-pong," according to the Windsor Collegiate teacher who first introduced the game to Ontario high schools in 1900.[31]

Having pronounced that jumping and other intensive physical activity posed health risks to women, doctors also addressed the question of accidental uterine displacement outside of sport. In the early 1920s, medical consultants for industrial compensation boards were required to evaluate claims that work-related accidents were responsible for uterine displacement. The wide-spread medical consensus was that an accident, *per se*, could not cause displacement. Thus, while some doctors still advised middle-class women to avoid vigorous sports, others asserted that jumping or falling posed no threat to the uterus. In one compensation case, for example, doctors accused a scrubwoman of malingering when she complained of uterine injury after a fall on the job.[32] The old class double standard was creating a new problem: how to convince women that heavy *work* was safe, while heavy *play* was dangerous.

If doctors and physical educators had examined the implications for jumping, research findings on "so-called traumatic displacements of the uterus" would have helped to dispel some of the myths surrounding women's athletics. But there is little evidence that the connection was made at this time. Criticism of doctors' faulty diagnoses and medical schools' obsolete training methods were made only in reference to the medical profession's obligations and career opportunities in the new field of industrial medicine. Although many women in the medical profession had advocated a more reasoned and scientific approach to questions of exercise and reproductive health, it was pressure from the business and industrial sectors that eventually brought about such dramatic changes on the displacement issue.[33]

THE MOTHERS OF TOMORROW

With mounting medical interest in the nation's wombs, it is not surprising that the health of girls as well as women attracted doctors' attention. One of the first manuals of physical education intended for a general, non-medical and non-teaching audience, written in the 1890s, was critical of parents who raised their daughters "like hot-house plants," forbidding them to join in the outdoor games that made their brothers healthy. It warned that, "when called upon to fulfil the functions of wives and mothers, their lives are made miserable by reason of suffering."[34]

Similarly, Tait McKenzie's textbook, *Exercise in Education and Medicine*, widely read from 1909 to the 1940s, advocated that girls follow a special physical training program designed to develop "those characteristics of growth, poise, speech, carriage and dress peculiar to [females]." However, McKenzie did not consider boys' outdoor games appropriate for girls, partly because after puberty, "their periods of temporary disability make them take less interest in active and competitive games."[35]

By the 1920s, it was not girls' and women's inactivity, but their over-exertion, that provoked medical censure. Still, the underlying "anatomy is destiny" rationale remained virtually unchanged. A 1929 statement on the dangers of Olympic competition for women contended that the development of beauty and femininity among young women was necessary "to attract the most worthy fathers for their children, provide the most healthful physiques for child-bearing and build the most maternal emotional and social behaviour patterns."[36] There was little, if any, evidence, however, that sport did *not* build "healthful physiques for child-bearing," or that it interfered with the reproductive process.[37]

Vitalist physiology continued to influence medical opinion and practice in sport gynecology long after it had been rejected in other areas. Although some doctors advocated exercise therapy in the early 1900s, a time when rest, not exercise, was the accepted medical treatment for virtually all diseases and injuries, they rarely made the connection between exercise therapy and women's full sporting participation.[38] For most doctors, unique female anatomy and physiology, embellished by social convention, constituted destiny. Ultimately, sporting competition at all levels, from intramural to Olympic, became the target of heated debate in medical and physical education circles.

The groundwork for the controversy was laid in the 1920s, but it was not until the 1930s that rhetoric was transformed into action. In 1930, when the American movement to abolish all women's athletic competition was reaching its peak, the first British Empire Games, held in Hamilton, Ontario, had thirty-three events in women's track and field, including the 200 metres.[39] At the Olympic level, however, the 200 metre and 800 metre events were eliminated on the grounds that they were too grueling for women. The broad jump and shot put were also cut: the first because of the alleged risk of displacement, and the second probably because it was excessively strenuous.

Sprinters Josie Dyment (left) and Myrtle Cook,
Toronto, 1926.

During this period, the health of adolescent boys and young men engaged in sport was also of medical interest, particularly as competition in school and university team sports and track events was flourishing. Doctors were concerned about the condition of the heart, as cardiac dilation and hypertrophy had been identified in several elite American and European athletes as early as 1913. Of course, it was rarely suggested that boys and men withdraw from sporting competition; most doctors simply warned against excesses and advocated shorter races for young boys.[40] Moreover, the "athlete's heart" issue prompted a series of studies designed to show the harmlessness of athletics for men. The slower pulse rate and greater cardiovascular efficiency of the athlete were eventually redefined as desirable, not as pathological states. Women were rarely the subjects of specific cardiovascular research at this time, although studies in the new field of exercise therapy had implications for female athletes.[41]

In the early 1900s, a number of German studies had recommended prenatal and postnatal exercise for women. Research in the postwar period reported that gymnastics and sports did not interfere with normal menstrual function in healthy women accustomed to physical exercise. Numerous articles on exercise therapy appeared in German journals in 1928, advocating gymnastics and exercise for physical and mental disorders as diverse as diabetes and insanity.[42]

A 1928 German study of 1,500 gymnasts found that the "exceptional [mental] strain" of competition — which the authors distinguished from "mere exercise" — had an "unfavourable" effect on menstruation in 27 percent of cases; conversely, performance suffered in 40 percent of cases during the menstrual period. The authors noted, however, that the 64 percent participation rate during menstruation was high, thereby indicating their low expectations. They concluded that healthy women accustomed to exercise may continue safely during menstruation, but advised against attempting to break records at this time. On the question of childbearing, both the German study and an earlier British survey of physical education college graduates found no relationship between difficult deliveries and sporting participation.[43]

The nineteenth-century medical position had held that female anatomy and physiology were suited only to the most gentle of

physical activities — except, of course, when the activity was domestic work. By the early decades of the twentieth century, some members of the medical profession were revising their views, censuring sedentary lifestyles and questioning the long-standing restrictions on women's physical activity. For the physicians who directed school and university physical education programs, the evidence was particularly convincing. Female sporting participation was growing and the health benefits were becoming well documented. Moreover, some women were challenging medical control of their reproductive health; they were not deterred from their sporting activities by predictions of displaced uteri or menstrual complications. But medical attitudes and practices were slow to change, and the competition controversy of the 1920s and 1930s gave new life to the medical monopoly over women's health.

Exercises with the chest expander,
from Edward Playter, "The Physical Culture of Women,"
in Benjamin Austin, ed., Woman: Her Character, Culture
and Calling (Brantford: Book and Bible House, 1898), p.232.

♦

Egg and spoon race at Hanlon's Point,
Toronto, 1907.

CHAPTER TWO

MAINTAINING MOTHERHOOD

MEDICAL SUPERVISION and control of all aspects of female sporting activities was firmly established by the turn of the century. Girls' and women's lives had been circumscribed by rigid definitions of sex-appropriate behaviour. However, sport threatened to blur the "natural" boundaries between the sexes. Most early medical opinion and practice on issues of women's health and physical activity owed more to intuition and ideology than to a scientific search for knowledge, and the more rigorous research that began around 1930 did not bring about instant enlightenment. Doctors have long viewed sportswomen as women first and athletes second. Therefore the conditions and injuries that preoccupy medical researchers are sex-specific rather than sport-specific. The female frailty myth proved and still proves to be extremely resistant to change.

The patriarchal view that woman's physical inferiority and reproductive vulnerability qualified her for special treatment and protection by men was seductive to both sexes. Maternal feminists in both the U.S.A. and Canada used this view of women to good political effect. They argued that women's unique capacity to "mother" qualified them for social reform work directed at working class and immigrant families. Therefore, the argument went, middle-class women must have the political power necessary to carry out this work: voting privileges, eligibility to run for public office, recognition before the law as "persons."[1] Yet this was not an argument based on equality, but on the moral superiority of women. As we will see, this strategy, applied to women's sport, served more to restrict than to liberate.

IT'S NOT IN WOMEN'S
NATURE TO COMPETE

Many of the medical issues in women's sport in the 1920s — uterine displacement, menstruation and pregnancy — converged in the controversy over sporting competition in the early 1930s. In the U.S.A., and to a lesser extent in Canada, it was not medical professionals but a small number of women in sport administration who took the initiative in this debate. They used conservative medical opinion to support their anti-competition stand. Although their goal — sport controlled by women for women — was obviously progressive, their rationale was based not on women's athletic competence, but on the old myths of female frailty and female moral superiority.

With the terms of this debate clouded by patriarchal ideology, it was obviously easier for a medical researcher to reiterate entrenched arguments against women's full participation than to prove the harmlessness of sport. Moreover, there was increasing societal demand on doctors to support the anti-competition side of the debate by addressing professional conferences or writing for the popular press on the health risks to girls and women. Thus, there was little need to marshal compelling arguments supported by rigorous scholarship; many audiences simply looked for the medical seal of approval on the common-sense belief that women's anatomy and physiology could not stand the strain of sporting competition. A 1938 magazine article, for example, cited "Dr. Lamb's sensible theory" to support a diatribe against "Amazon athletes."

There are numerous activities suitable for girls and women, but let these be of the type that will be suitable to their physical and mental natures... The tendency for girls to ape the activities of boys is regrettable. In most cases, it is physiologically and psychologically unsound and may be definitely harmful. [2]

Women's softball, Toronto, circa 1930.

To be fair, Lamb frequently stressed the value of sport for recreation and citizenship-building, and he also argued against specialization in boys' and men's sport. However, it was a common ploy for critics to soften their attacks with references to the evils of male sport and the moral superiority of women, warning women not to repeat men's horrible (but profitable) mistakes by professionalizing and commercializing team sports.

One New York physiologist, in a 1936 *Scientific American* article, argued that women's innate tendency to shun competition was partly responsible for their small numbers in the top ranks of athletes. Men, he claimed, are "more pugnacious and self-assertive."[3] Not only was intense physical activity beyond female capacity, according to this argument, but the competitive mentality was antithetical to her true nature. Physical director Agnes Wayman stated unequivocally in her 1934 text: "[The girl] is not or should not be interested primarily in making or breaking records." In a society that accorded a special, albeit subordinate place to women because of their alleged moral superiority and their transcendence of mere sporting victories, Wayman's advice was appropriate. Young women should engage in "activities which make for grace, poise, suppleness, quickness, agility, dexterity, beauty, general strength and endurance."[4]

Wayman also claimed that hospitals and sanitaria were "increasingly full of girls and women who will never be able to become mothers" on account of uterine displacement, "nervous diseases and other ailments" brought on by "the wrong sports."[5] These sweeping generalizations could be reported uncritically by a prominent physical education professor; yet the results of a sophisticated American study on the effects of landing shock in jumping for women never appeared in an American medical journal.[6] This research clearly demonstrated that jumping had negligible effects on the pelvic organs, and the author, C.H. McCloy, criticized "the largely non-medical group," especially conservative elderly women with little experience of jumping, who cited medical authorities in support of their opposition to women's sport. In fact, there was very little, very poor medical evidence of risk.[7]

Although physical education publications and popular magazines were rich sources of pseudo-medical wisdom, most medical journals presented equally conservative views. Doctors discussed exercise only in relation to middle-class women's reproductive health, failing to recognize that poverty, malnutrition, child abuse, wife abuse, and long hours in hazardous workplaces threatened the childbearing capacities of significantly larger numbers of girls and women.

... I am convinced of two things: (a) that physical activity is as good for women as it is for men; (b) that excess exercise is more harmful to women than to men ... It must of course be axiomatic that nothing can be good for a girl's body which renders her less capable of motherhood.

> Dr. Geoffrey Theobald,
> "Emancipation of Women,"
> *American Journal of Public Health*
> (September 1936): 871.

Winconsin physiologist, Percy Dawson, was one of the first to synthesize American, British and German research in his 1935 text, *The Physiology of Physical Education*. Although the findings were by no means conclusive, Dawson interpreted them conservatively, stressing, for example, "the care which should be expended in establishing normal menstruation" at puberty, and noting that unrestricted activity at this crucial stage of development frequently resulted in dysmenorrhea.[8] In fact, his overall position differed only minimally from the nineteenth-century myth of female frailty, a perspective also evident in his grouping in one chapter of women and girls, infants, children and young people, elderly persons, and the sick.

On the pregnancy issue, however, Dawson noted that exercise strengthened the body, enabling it to cope more easily with the additional weight. He also reported that most evidence indicated that strong abdominal muscles helped in childbirth, and that exercise did not necessarily cause rigid pelvic floor muscles. Yet, as late as the 1940s, doctors were claiming that these muscles were "especially thick and tense in tennis addicts and horse-women."[9] The muscle question gave rise to rather confused thinking, as doctors attempted to justify women's work and to restrict women's play. Since "nature" provided the basic muscular development for women's work and the involuntary muscles necessary for giving birth, so the argument went, it made good sense not to tamper with such admirable arrangements.

... feminine muscular development interferes with motherhood. What woman needs — and has — is a good system of involuntary muscles ... she has plenty of muscle and oxygen-carrying power for simple household tasks which take plenty of oxygen. She has ample development for a multitude of light office and factory work. But men should keep her away from the heavier tasks, both out of chivalry and good sense.

Dr. Donald Laird,
"Why Aren't More Women Athletes?"
Scientific American (March 1936): 143

Not all doctors opposed athletics for women; in fact, some coopted athletics in their exercise of power over women. One creative argument held that not only was "a girl accustomed to competitive sport" physically fit and well developed, but she was also more receptive to medical authority: "She obeys rules. She goes into training. She obeys the doctor ... as she would a coach." Typically treating women (of the appropriate race and class) as breeders, this male gynecologist added cheerfully, "My experience is that athletics for women is a fine thing for the race."[10]

That there might be white, middle-class women who preferred to remain unmarried and/or childless was inconceivable and unpardonable. Equally radical were those women who wanted to assume some control over the processes of pregnancy and birth. These women preferred to train and prepare for delivery for their own personal well-being and for the health of the infant, and not for the convenience of the gynecologist. The "Natural Childbirth" approach, as set out by British physiotherapist Jane Madders, involved understanding the birth process and practising muscle control to enable the woman "to accomplish her labour with the dignity and ease which come from knowledge and with training."[11]

AN AID FOR MENSTRUAL PAIN

One benefit of exercise widely accepted by North American doctors at this time was in the treatment of dysmenorrhea. Doctors had often linked "the current fashionable method of posture for girls" to health problems, specifically displacement of the abdominal viscera, and uterine displacement, with its attendant problems of dysmenorrhea and possible sterility. They blamed the young women (and, to a lesser extent, the young men) who were swayed by the "fickleness of changing fashion" without regard for the health risks.[12]

Similarly patronizing views were expressed by doctors conducting a posture correction program in a private women's college in Georgia. They claimed that students responded well "without their being conscious of what is going on within them." Thus, it was just as effective to promise "beauty, health and efficiency" through swimming and dancing as it was to present formal lectures on posture. The annual college health campaign culminated in the "Miss Health" contest; the finalists paraded "barefooted" in "dark bathing suits" before the judges in typical Beauty Queen style. Candidates were chosen for their good medical records, which were checked for general health, colds, weight, feet, posture, carriage and menstrual periods.[13]

Clearly, the monitoring of menstrual periods served a social-control function, as well; pregnancy was hardly compatible with the title of *Miss* Health. Moreover, the implication that irregularly menstruating students were also disqualified reveals the perceived links between health and the *potential* for motherhood. Such invasions of students' privacy were not, however, unusual. In 1930, the women's physical director at the University of Minnesota warned teachers that the rule forbidding basketball playing during the first three days of menstruation was not always enforceable through the commonly used honour system. Therefore, she recommended that the coach "take the initiative in speaking to the girls"; obviously, the coach was a woman.[14] Male coaches could not properly make such inquiries. However, one Ontario athlete recalled her male coaches' hesitant approach to the "menstruation issue" when she was training in the early 1930s: "They wouldn't ask you right out, of course, and if they did in those days, we probably wouldn't know what the word meant!" Instead, they asked pointed questions such as "Do you want to practise today?" or "How are you today?"[15]

The need for corrective programs prompted one Illinois physical education director to establish a special restricted curriculum for "temporarily excused girls, which includes temporary disability and menstrual excuses," while another teacher designed a program of relaxation exercises and activities "to be an aid during the menstrual period": ping-pong, archery and ring toss.[16]

During the 1930s and 1940s, doctors continued to follow Clelia Mosher's lead in developing specific exercises for the treatment of dysmenorrhea. The Mosher exercises, as they were called, were designed to strengthen the abdominal muscles, and were prescribed up to the 1960s. Similarly, exercises developed by a Navy surgeon, H.E. Billig, in 1942 were intended to stretch pelvic ligaments which became constricted during menstruation. Whereas Mosher's primary purpose had been to relieve women's menstrual suffering, Billig and his colleagues in the medical department of a San Diego aircraft factory were interested only in developing "an effective method of reducing absentee hours" in order to maintain production for the war effort.[17]

Beneficial effects were attributed to both the Mosher and Billig exercises in the majority of cases, although one doctor advised caution in interpreting these results. Swayed, no doubt, by the view that menstrual suffering was imaginary, he warned that "cures" were also susceptible to "suggestion," when women were in "a highly nervous and emotional state."[18] Evidently, both the condition and its relief were "all in their heads."

A few doctors continued to test the Mosher and Billig exercises up to the 1960s, using high school and college students as subjects. Some modifications were recommended, but the basic

Girls' Y.W.C.A. calisthenics class, Manitoba, 1929.

principle that increased abdominal strength and trunk flexibility alleviated the symptoms of dysmenorrhea continued to hold true.[19] Most doctors, however, recommended these therapeutic exercises as part of a physical education program, rather than identifying sports and games which developed strength and flexibility in the abdominal and pelvic areas. The latter approach would have had the effect of promoting female sporting participation, rather than weighing down the physical education program with corrective or therapeutic components relevant only to a few students with dysmenorrhea.

The emphasis on posture in young women's physical education programs continued, but by the 1950s and 1960s menstrual health was rarely the rationale. In one Toronto high school, Posture Week, first organized by the girls' physical education teachers in 1954, concluded with a Tea Dance and the crowning of the Posture Queen. As the school yearbook wryly reported, the project "improved the posture of the students for one week."

Yet a report of the event, with photographs, was published in a major Toronto newspaper on at least one occasion. Girls' sport rarely, if ever, received such coverage.[20]

AN ACCIDENT OF THE CALENDAR

Throughout this century, doctors have continued to investigate whether girls and women should be "allowed" to take part in sport and physical activity during menstruation. The ubiquitous advice literature on this topic warned women to exercise caution, by modifying or foregoing physical activities at least during the first days of the period. By the 1960s, however, doctors were turning their attention to new sport gynecology issues. Perhaps, after almost a century they had recognized the futility of their efforts; women did not feel compelled to seek the medical seal of approval for every detail of their lifestyles.

For elite female athletes, the issue of supervision and control of menstruation was somewhat different. The alleged disadvantage suffered by the high performance athlete whose period coincided with an important competition posed a new challenge to medical professionals. Had menstruation not been viewed as disabling, however, the issue probably would not have arisen.

Following the 1932 Los Angeles Olympics, some doctors experimented with hormone treatments to delay the period. No negative effects were reported, but one Norwegian physician included this topic in his discussion of doping and noted the unknown risks associated with hormone use.[21] This practice received relatively little medical attention, although it continued until the 1960s when oral contraceptives allowed hormonal control of the entire menstrual cycle.[22]

Until the 1960s, there was little conclusive evidence that performance was adversely affected by menstruation, other than the obvious disadvantage of dysmenorrhea. A complicating factor concerned the interrelation of physiological and psychological effects. The warnings issued by doctors, coaches, parents and teachers obviously predisposed some women to avoid maximum exertion during menstruation. There were corresponding drops in performance. One isolated 1937 study reported a drop in psychomotor coordination both before and during the period.[23]

Women were warned against competing during "the unstable premenstrual and intramenstrual phases, when powers of concentration, sharpness of the sensorial perceptions and speed of reactions are reduced, which signifies a mental readiness for accidents."[24] These allegations of mental lapses were indistinguishable from the old myths of mental instability associated with the menstrual cycle. Premenstrual symptoms and dysmenorrhea did affect a small percentage of women. However, by restricting the sporting activities of all women on these grounds, doctors showed a cavalier disregard for evidence provided by the athletes themselves.[25]

The issue of swimming during menstruation had been somewhat hypothetical before the introduction of the tampon in the 1930s. Many women no doubt did not swim during the time of heavy menstrual flow for practical reasons. One study reported discomfort due to extremes of temperature among a few women who swam during menstruation; such findings probably accounted for the advice to girls, in a book distributed by Kotex in the 1940s, to avoid baths or showers that were too hot or too cold.[26] Most studies simply took for granted the prohibition against swimming, and did not investigate its effects.

There was, predictably, considerable medical interest in the safety and effectiveness of tampons by the early 1940s, when, according to some surveys, tampons were used by up to 25 percent of women.[27] Advertising for tampons, of course, stressed the freedom to swim and play games. But most gynecologists were more interested in the moral and health effects than in the liberating potential for sportswomen. As late as 1945, doctors noted the possibility of "rhythmic play of pressure against surfaces uniquely alert to erotic feeling" — i.e. the clitoris. Clearly, masturbation phobia had not yet disappeared.[28]

Nor were gynecologists entirely satisfied with the principle of intravaginal protection, which required women to become familiar with, and even to handle, a part of their anatomy previously considered male and/or medical territory. Thus, tampons with applicators were recommended, since "contamination" of the vagina was unavoidable when using other types.[29] Tampax advertisements in the 1940s stressed the convenience of the "dainty applicators": "hands need not touch the Tampax at all" (or, it implied, the vagina).[30]

By 1965, doctors and physical educators were in general agreement on the "health benefits of wholesome exercise" for girls and women, and were questioning whether forced abstention from any sporting activity during the menstrual period was necessary. Ironically, the same kinds of surveillance proposed in the 1930s to confirm the absence of "menstrual problems" were recommended in the 1950s to determine whether "menstrual excuses" were really valid.[31]

Most research findings supported the more progressive approach. In one study of high school swimmers, those who continued swimming during menstruation reported no negative effects, and members of a synchronized swimming team who trained and competed throughout the menstrual cycle experienced less menstrual discomfort than students who swam only as part of the physical education program. There was no evidence that swimming caused variations in the menstrual cycle.[32]

Elite athletes were subjected to medical scrutiny for different reasons. In 1978, when the issue of hormonal control of athletes' cycles was discussed at an international sportsmedicine conference, one doctor recommended oral contraceptives or, in emergencies, oral progesterone, to postpone menstruation during competition; he implied that this was desirable for all female athletes. Although doping was a major ethical issue in competitive sport, menstrual control was not classified as doping; the alternative — competing while disadvantaged by menstruation — was simply "an accident of the calendar."[33]

Medical control of the menstrual cycle was not new, but the stated purpose had invariably been the maintenance of fertility and reproductive health. Whenever sport and menstruation had proved incompatible, the medical solution had been to control or curtail sporting participation, rather than to intervene in the menstrual cycle. Thus it is not surprising that this particular hormone treatment, intended to maximize athletic performance rather than motherhood potential, was not a popular subject of medical research. Moreover, while intervention to improve the performance of the country's top female athletes could be justified on nationalistic grounds, the possibility that "ordinary women" might use these techniques for less worthy purposes was obviously a concern.

It was, therefore, ironic that two "natural" outcomes of intensive physical training — delayed menarche and amenorrhea — freed athletes from the vicissitudes of the menstrual cycle and were welcomed by many women. The onset of menstruation at the expected age and the regular appearance of the menstrual period until menopause are two visible indicators of a woman's fertility that have long been under medical scrutiny. Pregnancy and childbirth are, of course, the ultimate proof of fertility, but as birth control methods have become increasingly accessible, pregnancy has, to some extent, become a matter of choice for many women. Menarche, menstruation and menopause, although controllable hormonally, are nevertheless inevitable. Thus, delayed menarche and amenorrhea in female athletes have attracted more attention in sportsmedicine in the past two decades than any other women's health issue.

NORMAL BODILY FUNCTIONS

The timing of menarche has long absorbed physiologists and others concerned with human development, but the relation between intensive training and delayed menarche was not investigated until the 1970s. (A 1941 study noted a later age of menarche among physical education students than among university students in general, but the difference was explained in terms of body type: those with linear physiques matured later than those with lateral physiques.[34]) Around 1969, Rose Frisch and her Harvard colleagues developed the critical fatness theory, proposing a direct causal relationship between body weight and menarche; lean body mass and body fat were identified as the factors controlling the endocrine changes of puberty. Frisch's later research also linked these factors to the maintenance of menstrual cycles. The high incidence of amenorrhea among ballet dancers, runners and women with anorexia nervosa (an eating problem producing extreme weight loss) resulted from low fat/lean ratios.[35]

The critical fatness hypothesis was the subject of much medical debate. Whereas Frisch's model relied on external, environmental factors as triggers, a popular alternative was based on internal, biological factors, specifically developmental changes in the endocrine system. Thus, the debate mirrored the classic environment vs. heredity argument.[36] Frisch suggested that hard work, malnutrition and poor living conditions were responsible for temporary periods of infertility in some populations. Thus, if a higher birthrate was the goal, the remedy was external and economic, rather than internal and biological. The alternative explanation located the causes of delayed menarche or amenorrhea within the individual woman's "genetic programming." This theory was more compatible with the traditional medical model that viewed female health problems as functions of female anatomy and physiology, while ignoring the gender, class and race divisions of the wider social context. Subsequent research suggests that a single-factor explanation is unlikely to account for all variations in reproductive functioning.

The attention generated by these issues was related, of course, to the medical concern that permanent sterility would result from strenuous training, although there was no support for this concern. By the late 1970s, a considerably higher incidence of amenorrhea was recorded. Of the sixty-six participants in the 1964 Olympics studied by Ekaterina Zaharieva, only one had been amenorrheic, whereas about 50 percent of American rowers and swimmers in the 1976 Olympics experienced amenorrhea.[37] The escalating rate was related, in part, to women's increasingly strenuous training schedules. The American study showed that the incidence of menstrual variations increased in proportion to the hours trained. As well, women's growing participation in distance running, which required several hours of training daily, probably contributed to this trend. A 1977 study of American women on collegiate track and cross-country teams showed that between 6 percent and 43 percent experienced amenorrhea, with rates varying in direct relation to weekly mileage.[38]

Reviewing the research on distance running and women's general and reproductive health, the American College of Sports Medicine issued an Opinion Statement in 1979 supporting full female participation in distance events.[39] Whereas 1928 medical opinion had been partly responsible for limiting women's Olympic events to 200 metres, the 1979 statement was partly responsible for the inclusion of a women's marathon in the 1984 Olympics.

> ... Females should not be denied the opportunity to compete in long-distance running. There exists no conclusive scientific or medical evidence that long-distance running is contraindicated for the healthy, trained female athlete. The American College of Sports Medicine recommends that females be allowed to compete at the national and international level in the same distances in which their male counterparts compete.
>
> American College of Sports Medicine Opinion Statement, in Kenneth Dyer, *Challenging the Men* (St. Lucia, Queensland: University of Queensland Press, 1982), p. 240.

The high media profile of the fitness industry and the women's movement no doubt account for increased coverage of athletes' gynecological health in all major sportsmedicine, gynecology, endocrinology, science, biology and physical education journals. The vast majority of articles treated menstrual variations as a problem, their authors obviously sharing the nineteenth-century conviction that the twenty-eight day cycle is the norm and motherhood the destiny for all women. Rarely was it suggested that a young woman might wish to weigh the possible costs of intensive training against child-bearing potential, and to make an informed decision regarding her future.

Doctors writing in the mass media rarely acknowledged that one could not generalize from findings based on a small, non-representative sample of top female athletes on Olympic training regimens. Nor did they admit that the scientific findings were inconclusive and speculative. By the 1980s, sport gynecologists' conservatism permeated the mass media in much the same way as the scanty evidence of the 1920s had been marshaled and popularized as medical legitimation for restricted female participation in sport.

In contrast to the mass media, medical literature of the early 1980s showed signs of a more sophisticated, holistic approach to sport gynecology issues. A 1981 editorial in the *Journal of the American Medical Association* stated that "a complex interplay of physical, hormonal, nutritional, psychological and environmental factors" was responsible for delayed menarche and changes in menstrual function among athletes.[40] The debate over the relative importance of biological and environmental factors, however, was seldom reported outside medical journals.

Typical review articles on this subject for non-medical audiences, however, presented generalizations that were both misleading and alarming.[41] Their shortcomings did not escape criticism, although it was an anthropologist, Robert Malina, not a physiologist or a gynecologist, who objected to articles of this kind. He pointed out that non-biological factors, such as family size and social class, should not be overlooked. Furthermore, he challenged the claim that early training delayed maturation, and suggested that some girls began or continued training because they were late maturers, and had more time to perfect their athletic skills before pubertal changes in physique interfered with their performance. Swimming, according to Malina, was one of the few sports in which the late-maturing physique was a disadvantage; the mature female body was better suited to swimming.[42]

However, Malina did not pursue the obvious implication: if puberty represents the end of many girls' sporting careers, it is probably the sport, rather than the female physique, that is inappropriate for lifetime participation. Success in most sports depends on strength and endurance. Whereas a boy grows into his childhood sports as his height, weight and muscular strength increase, a girl tends to grow out of her sports at puberty when her breasts and hips develop and her body fat level increases. If late-maturing athletes are indeed a small, self-selected, non-representative group of survivors, then studies of this group contribute little to understanding the general physiology of physically active girls and women.

By 1983, the term "exercise-associated amenorrhea" had developed a high profile.[43] Many doctors continued to believe that any menstrual variation merited medical supervision and/or intervention, even though there was growing evidence that regular cycles returned when exercise levels were reduced. Mona Shangold, a widely read New York gynecologist, maintained that amenorrhea in athletes should be investigated as thoroughly as in non-athletes, with a "thorough gynecologic-endocrine evaluation including examination and laboratory tests."[44]

Sportsmedicine articles and advice columns, increasingly common in sport/recreation and women's magazines, often took a personal and subjective approach to the amenorrhea issue.[45] The medical experts who expounded their views in these publications tended to represent the most conservative medical opinion, while more progressive doctors encountered barriers to publishing in both the medical literature and the mass media. Some doctors agreed, however, that amenorrhea required medical attention only if the woman wished to conceive, and observed that sportswomen often welcomed the temporary cessation of menstruation during peak training. A few even voiced the radical notion that regular menstruation was "abnormal," a relatively recent evolutionary development as humans became a sedentary species; they argued that it was more logical to treat delayed menarche and menstrual variations as the rule, and not the exception, among female athletes.[46] Yet a 1982 letter in the *New England Journal of Medicine* reported two cases of amenorrheic women (joggers) who did not conceive after taking fertility drugs. They did so only after they stopped their regular jogging program.[47] The *Toronto Star* apparently found this item newsworthy, announcing "Heavy Jogging Hurts Ovulation Doctor Reports."[48] With the association between exercise and amenorrhea established for more than a decade, and the relationship between ovulation and menstruation understood for considerably longer, these findings were not particularly surprising.

A New York trichologist (hair care authority) discussed the alleged association between physical activity, "disrupted" menstrual cycles, "hormonal disturbances" and hair loss in women. Warning against "overdoing" physical fitness by "repeatedly pushing your body beyond its natural physical limit," the author identified not only athletes, but also "successful career women" as frequent sufferers of hormone changes and hair loss.[49]

Medical reaction to a 1983 article in the *New England Journal of Medicine* on the personalities of male "obligatory runners" is illuminating. The authors, themselves runners, proposed a similarity between anorexic women and obligatory runners in character, adaptive styles and backgrounds. The women viewed dieting as a means of achieving the cultural ideal of beauty through thinness; the men saw running as a demonstration of athletic prowess, commonly associated with vocational and sexual effectiveness. Many anorexic women were compulsively athletic, and the obligatory runners often displayed a preoccupation with food and thinness.[50] Not surprisingly, some male doctors took offence at this thesis, resenting the alleged implication that all male runners were mentally ill and destined to become anorexic. Needless to say, not one challenged the authors' assumptions concerning the personality disorders of anorexic women; apparently, women's extreme attempts to live up to cultural ideals are pathological, while men's are simply idiosyncratic.[51]

The high profile of amenorrhea and similar sex-specific, exercise-related problems reflected opposition to women's sporting activity, conservatism in the medical profession and sensationalist journalism on women's issues. One Minnesota researcher noted that the medical community tended to look at risks first and benefits second, whereas researchers in the running community took the opposite approach.[52] But this theory did not explain why much of the conservative medical opinion came from doctors who were serious runners, nor did it account for the outdated and alarmist advice directed exclusively at women and exemplified, as late as 1983, by the medical instruction to female runners to "take the precaution of special exercises to strengthen crotch muscles and thus ward off any danger of fallen uteruses."[53]

The lingering effects of the female frailty myth were seen in the medical and public preoccupation with sex-specific rather than sport-specific conditions and injuries. Although many sportsmedicine researchers questioned the old assumptions concerning fertility and menstrual function, more progressive views were slow to appear in the mass media.

♦

Doris Craig in the uniform of the Lakeside Ladies' Athletic Club, Toronto, 1925.

CHAPTER THREE

PERFECTING WOMANHOOD
THROUGH SPORT

WOMEN'S SPORTING PARTICIPATION during the past century has been constrained by the forces of patriarchal control over female sexuality. As we have seen, doctors attempted to classify as inappropriate any sporting activity which allegedly jeopardized female reproductive health. Only belatedly did they demonstrate some flexibility on the question. Doctors were not alone in their endeavour; they were aided by educators, clergy and other guardians of moral order and male hegemony. In addition, twentieth-century developments in psychology and psychiatry expanded the ideological ground controlled by medical professionals, as female sexuality became differentiated from the reproductive function that had formerly been the focus of medical attention.

Since most sporting activities take place in public, the spectacle of women at play has long been a popular media target. We have seen that doctors who expressed their views in the mass media tended to represent the most conservative medical opinion on issues of women and sport. Journalists, educators, physical education directors and, more recently, fitness specialists helped to perpetuate in print the "loss of femininity" myth and the dichotomy between "masculine" and "feminine" sports. In practical terms, they either blamed masculine sports for making female athletes unfeminine, or accused participants of being masculine at the outset. Most medical and educational professionals displayed the same sexist and heterosexist biases as journalists, alleging that non-conforming sportswomen were intent on imitating men, or were lesbian. The accessibility of this kind of "expert" opinion served to entrench the moral leadership of white upper-class males.

Early in the century, when the physiological capacity for mothering and "maternal instinct" were seen as key components of "true womanhood," medical pronouncements directed women towards sporting activities that promoted general and reproductive health and that fostered the feminine attributes of grace and agility, charm and passivity. By the 1960s, however, the moral prescriptions that had accompanied medical advice in the preceding half-century were rarely seen, but the attitudes and practices of gynecologists, physiologists and other medical professionals continued to reflect and reinforce patriarchal ideology. Moreover, the victim-blaming orientation of psychiatric practice upheld medical control over female sexuality. Mental health authorities were empowered to define and label sexual/moral "deviance," and psychologists' preoccupation with female athletes' sex-role identity and alleged role conflict perpetuated the old myths of inherent incompatibilities between sport and femininity.

Adrienne Rich identifies heterosexuality as a political institution and "a beachhead of male dominance." She argues that alternatives in sexual preference and practice constitute important avenues of resistance to institutionalized compulsory heterosexuality.[1] Rich's claims are particularly relevant to a discussion of women and sport; the attitudes and practices surrounding the sexual identity and the sexual orientation of female athletes are central to the analysis presented here.

As the dominant sex, men rewarded — and continue to reward — female athletes who satisfied stereotyped heterosexual standards of femininity in their appearance and in the performance of their sport. As in other social contexts, women's femininity served to validate male identity and both individual and collective male power. A woman's conformity to male-defined standards of heterosexual attractiveness signifies her acquiescence to men's rules, as she competes with other women for the attention and protection of men.

Thus, femininity is predicated on weakness, dependence and individuality. Not simply an aesthetic, it is both a symbol and an enactment of women's subordinate status.[2] In sport, therefore, the femininity of women who play traditionally male sports is suspect unless they make deliberate efforts to meet male-defined standards of attractiveness and to assert their heterosexual orientation. Women who do not comply draw male censure, not for their sporting performance — which may elicit admiration — but for the threat they pose to male supremacy by putting personal achievement ahead of femininity.

Heterosexist attitudes and practices determine the classification of sports as feminine and masculine. The rules of male-dominated sports systems have long excluded women from certain sports and dictated the quality and degree of all female sporting involvement. To a lesser extent, the masculine/feminine dichotomy excludes males from certain activities and casts doubt on the heterosexuality of those males who do participate. Clearly, without the legitimizing force of compulsory heterosexuality, this classification would founder; a sporting activity would be feminine simply by virtue of female involvement, not by reason of its alleged compatibility with the ideals of femininity or heterosexual appeal.

Social class also affects the way compulsory heterosexuality is applied in sport. There are class differences in parental tolerance towards "sissies" or "tomboys," for example. Corresponding degrees of sex differentiation in children's play and in choice of sports can also be partially attributed to class. Furthermore, the attributes of femininity and feminine sports are not constant across class lines. For example, one form of women's riding, dressage, is an activity of the privileged class, while another, rodeo, has rural, working class roots. The equestrienne is considered feminine, but the rodeo rider is not.

Recreational and leisure activities, as well as competitive sports, maintain compulsory heterosexuality, and they, too, are subject to class differences. Certain activities have a long tradition of segregated or male-only participation; others are played jointly by both sexes. However, these systems of classification have developed in specific social and historical contexts,

with the result that single-sex participation in certain activities —
such as pleasure skating, softball and bowling — may be
acceptable in certain settings, but may be viewed as a rejection of
the heterosexual norm in others.[3]

Regardless of social class, however, men have usually been
able to exclude women from their leisure pursuits without
jeopardizing their heterosexual reputations. Through a strange
twist of logic, the all-male fishing, hunting or boating trip
enhances men's heterosexual identity. It is male participation in
traditionally female activities — dance or synchronized swimming
— that suggests male (but not female) homosexuality. Consider
the female equivalent to a hunting trip: women travel to an
isolated area, live together for several days and develop strong
emotional ties through their joint enjoyment of a recreational
activity. Unless the women were visiting a health and beauty spa
or "diet farm," there is little doubt that this activity would
threaten the heterosexual norm.

The second major link between sport and heterosexuality is
the socializing value attached to sporting participation. Throughout the century, men have utilized the bonding that is a
byproduct of sporting experience to maintain their dominant
status and to strengthen male alliances across class lines. It is
rarely alleged that such camaraderie fosters homosexual tendencies; friendships forged on the playing field have inspired
masterpieces of male rhetoric concerning the manliness of those
involved.[4] Such ties, however, when developed among girls or
women, were treated quite differently by commentators. Before
the 1930s, they were virtually ignored; more recently, however,
many attempts to discredit female solidarity have been based on
allegations of lesbianism.

Qualities such as loyalty, cooperation and solidarity — the
essence of team sports — were hardly compatible with the
isolation and competition between women that characterized the
femininity game and the wife-and-mother role. Moreover,
women's capacity for support and nurturing was recognized and
rewarded only when the beneficiaries were very young or very
old, or sick, or male. Supportive relationships between women,
benefitting women, are a clear threat to male supremacy.

LADY CYCLISTS, NOT MANNISH WOMEN

Although the notion of femininity throughout the past century consistently encompassed reproductive capacity, sexual identity and presentation of self as female, the relative significance and concrete manifestations of each component varied as attitudes and practices changed. One must therefore consider these concepts within specific historical contexts.

During the late nineteenth and early twentieth centuries, femininity was inseparable from motherhood. Maternal feminists believed that the special contribution that women could make to society rested on their innate capacity to "mother." Even women as radical as Canadian suffragist Nellie McClung expressed a profound belief in maternal instinct. McClung did admit, however, that existing social conditions made marriage and motherhood a less than perfect option for many women. She criticized male moralists who advocated large families while failing to improve the lives of those already born.[5]

Cycling attire of the 1890s.

Although motherhood inspired considerable rhetoric, other aspects of female sexuality were rarely discussed. In practical terms, too, female sexuality was mystified, for women's legs and pelvic area were hidden under voluminous skirts. The concealing skirt also had symbolic importance for male/female relationships: it signified that the wearer, being morally superior, had taken responsibility for man's lack of sexual self-control, and had removed all sexual stimulus from his sight. If she wore revealing clothes, she could expect to be blamed for the consequences. Needless to say, what constituted a temptation in women's dress changed dramatically between the Victorian matron and the twenties flapper.

Up to the turn of the century, female temptations included the ankles and legs. The dress reformers advocating the bloomer, and the sportswomen, especially cyclists, adopting it in the 1880s and 1890s, met with widespread criticism. Some Toronto school trustees censured "all female teachers who have been riding bicycles in male attire, commonly called 'bloomers'."[6] One Toronto critic held these women responsible for "unholy desires on the part of boys and men."

> ... one girl in a bloomer costume will create far greater and more widespread corruption among boys than a city full of show bills, so will a well developed girl in short dresses. [7]

The associations between dress reformers, women's rights advocates and "lady cyclists" did not go unnoticed. Each group overstepped women's private domestic sphere and challenged patriarchal hegemony. Some critics accused these women of imitating men, yet few men viewed this as flattery. Both politics and sport, by their public nature and their long tradition of male participation, were unequivocally masculine pursuits. The wearing of "male attire" (i.e. any deviation from the skirt) confirmed that these "modern mannish maidens" were abandoning "the 'old sweet ways' of womanhood."[8] Not surprisingly, the male beneficiaries of the "old sweet ways" denounced these trends as selfish, frivolous and immoral.

Although it was the proper attire for "moral" women, the skirt did not hinder sexual access as the much criticized bloomer did. If

Fashion plates of the 1890s, from J.W. Smithson, "Corsets — The Curse of Modern Civilization," Physical Culture 3 (July 1900), p.156.

protection, or even health, rather than concealment and adornment, had been a function of women's clothing, skirts would have been replaced by some form of pants long before the twentieth century. McClung was one of the few to recognize this inconsistency. She based her argument for dress reform not on health considerations, as did most of her female and male contemporaries, but on the political implications of women's fashion.

> The absurdly tight skirts which prevented the wearer from walking like a human being, made a pitiful cry to the world. They were no doubt worn as a protest against the new movement among women, which has for its object the larger liberty, the larger humanity of women. The hideous mincing gait of the tightly-skirted woman seems to speak. It said: "I am not a useful human being — see! I cannot walk — I dare not run, but I am a woman — I have my sex to commend me. I am not of use. I am made to be supported. My sex is my only appeal.
>
> Nellie McClung,
> *In Times Like These*
> (1915; Toronto: University of
> Toronto Press, 1972), p. 62

McClung no doubt understood that "the larger liberty, the larger humanity of women" threatened some women, as long as there remained a protected, but subordinate, niche for those who presented their bodies as sexual assets and physical liabilities. If merely walking "like a human being" detracted from the feminine image, then clearly an activity like running or cycling was anathema.

The women who defended rational dress and physical activity usually relied on well-established health and beauty arguments, rather than the unpopular idea that women had as much right to practical clothing and leisure activities as men.[9] One "lady cyclist" felt compelled to remind readers that she was, after all, still a "lady," welcoming male assistance in changing tires, negotiating steep hills or dealing with cows on the road.[10]

Most women writing about sport and physical activity in the early 1900s were similarly apologetic, assuring readers that physical training "need not convert [a girl] into a mannish woman," nor would it render her "unattractive to men," since the ability to "endure material hardships" improved her chances in this regard, presumably by preparing her for the harsh realities of married life.[11] Another journalist dismissed athletics for women, claiming that they "need not rashly bestride the bicycle nor rush through the non-productive drill of the gymnasium," when housework offered precisely the same health benefits.[12]

[Sweeping] a heavy carpet has long been advocated — by those who never do it — as a healthy and stimulating pastime ...Personally, if I went into that kind of thing for health-and-beauty's sake, I should choose the regular gymnasium and "its scientific instructor."

Woman's Sphere,
Canadian Magazine
(September 1903): 469-70.

Yet women were rarely in a position to change the terms of the debate; they were usually reacting and defending rather than proposing new and radical directions for women's physical activity. Although a growing number of women held university posts as directors of women's physical education by the turn of the century, most were subordinate to the male physical director, often a former medical man with rather fixed views on women's physical activity. Powerlessness was not the only problem. The primacy of the femininity ideal was rarely challenged, even by progressive and influential women in physical education. Most shared Ethel Cartwright's position that "girls should be impressed with the fact that physical education does not strive to make them men's physical equal, but it aims at perfecting their womanhood."[13]

Physical educator Benarr MacFadden was one of the few advocates of women's physical activity who did not use femininity or preparation for motherhood as rationales. His periodical, *Physical Culture*, stressed the ideals of strength and beauty through physical activity. According to MacFadden, there should be "but very slight difference between the strength of man and woman." He attributed "the proverbial feminine weakness" to "the conventional skirt, the bigoted prejudice of parents against play of a romping nature and . . . the terrible corset."[14]

Some advocates of women's athletics voiced the same concerns that parents (presumably of the middle class) raised daughters like "hothouse plants," restricting them to indoor activities such as piano practice while their brothers were enjoying outdoor play.[15] Class differences were rarely identified explicitly, although they were no doubt an important factor. Yet sweat and strain remained acceptable for working women but unfeminine when they appeared on the faces of "ladies."

THE DEMANDS OF WOMANLY PROPRIETY

While early twentieth-century definitions of femininity permitted heterosexual appeal of a discreet nature, they did not preclude close relationships between women. The ideas on homosexuality developed by Kraft-Ebbing, Havelock Ellis and Freud had limited impact in North America until the 1920s; previously, intense emotional relationships between women had been considered both legitimate and "normal." In the late nineteenth century, as careers opened up in higher education and in the professions, increasing numbers of women recognized the

"A *Suitable Dress for Girls,*"
from *Strathcona Trust,* Syllabus of Physical Exercises for
Schools *(Toronto: Copp Clark, 1911), p.164.*

Women's hockey, Toronto, 1912.

impossibility of combining this work with marriage and mother-hood and chose not to marry. The support that these women offered one another, either in private romantic friendship or in academic and professional milieux, was crucial to their survival in a society which devalued women's intellectual ability.[16]

In the women's colleges and universities in the northeastern United States and in eastern Canada, rowing and tennis, basket-ball and field hockey were offered to female students before the turn of the century, primarily as health-promoting exercise. There is no evidence that participation in these sports, or the resulting enjoyment and camaraderie, were subjects of sexual innuendo. In fact, the social values were usually subordinated to the benefits to reproductive health. A gymnastic display by female students at McGill University in 1896 caused a Montreal journalist to enthuse: "It encourages faith in the future of the country that will be able to draw from so bright-eyed, healthy-bodied, clean-limbed a host, for the mothers of a coming generation."[17]

The late nineteenth-century moralists who agonized about the degeneracy of youth in the sporting context were primarily concerned with interaction between young men and women. One critic, for example, alleged that a girl on a bicycle had only one purpose in mind — to associate with boys: "... on her bicycle she can at the same time satisfy her taste for boys' society and satisfy the demands of propriety" (as could young women who went ice skating with men).[18]

There is little evidence that such moralizing deterred female cyclists and skaters, any more than it stopped young working-class women from frequenting dance halls and cinemas during the war years. Whatever the context, it was the mingling of the sexes, not women's homosocial activities, that elicited this kind of censure. This relative tolerance for single-sex sport and leisure activities did not, of course, signify that compulsory hetero-sexuality was dormant, for the emphasis on femininity and preparation for motherhood characterized most rationales of women's sport. Moreover, the pejorative term "tomboy" was in popular use, as it had been for almost four centuries. This term was directed at "a girl who behaves like a spirited or boisterous boy," although the dictionary defined "spirited" as "animated" and "courageous," characteristics which would seem desirable for the male or female personality.[19] For a brief time, during Gold Rush days, "tomboy" was a complimentary term for a woman who could do a man's work.[20]

By the early twentieth century, "hybrid tomboyism" threat-ened "to disturb the seemliness, the dignity, the attractiveness, the lustre" of womanhood. According to one critic, it was in woman's "sweetness, her weakness, her lovingness" that her "divinity" lay. To redefine weakness as strength was masterly; clearly, it was the existing balance of power between the sexes that tomboyism threatened to disturb.[21] One positive note was provided by Benarr MacFadden, who asserted that, almost without exception, beautiful women were "tomboys" in their youth: "They ran, wrestled, climbed trees" and subsequently developed "beautiful symmetry of muscles."[22] Yet, whatever effect tomboyism may have had on heterosexual appeal, the term simply signified a certain set of behaviours. It was not until the

1960s that it was used to connote innate and immutable traits that were allegedly incompatible with femininity and hetero-sexuality.

FREE TO BE A FLAPPER

By the First World War, attitudes and practices relating to female sexuality were changing. The emergency required that women work in areas of employment formerly reserved for men, a move that necessitated some changes in social relations between the sexes. The postwar years marked a new openness regarding sexuality and a corresponding relaxing of dress codes, especially for women.

During the 1920s and early 1930s, women's sport probably enjoyed more extensive newspaper coverage and attracted larger crowds than at any other period in the past century.[23] In this "Golden Age," critics who espoused the "loss of femininity" argument were temporarily silenced, perhaps because the well-chosen pictures of sportswomen appearing in newspapers and periodicals confirmed their feminine appearance.[24] Moreover,

Women's baseball team, Biscotasing Ontario, 1921.

acceptable clothing for sporting activities was no longer as distinctive as it had been at the turn of the century. The bloomer had evolved into the popular track pants and shorts, and athletes' clothing was not incompatible with the fashionably feminine, boyish look of the flapper. The twenties marked the beginning of the "fashionalization" of sports clothing. As one fashion writer observed in 1928, "Today, fashion decrees that sports' clothes and especially bathing suits must be practical as well as decorative."[25] For many years the onus had been on sportswomen to make their innovative attire decorative as well as practical.

Yet the lighter, less restrictive clothing of the flapper era did not escape criticism. Some doctors blamed these styles for the high incidence of tuberculosis and other diseases among young women. Moreover, as moral guardians of society, the wearers were still blamed for corrupting hapless males, in particular "that fine type of Canadian manhood," the military man.[26]

Despite such criticism, active girls and women enjoyed more freedom in dress, as long as they restricted the wearing of sports clothes to the appropriate private setting. Much of the controversy over women's sporting competition stemmed from the alleged impropriety of public track meets, swimming contests and basketball games, where young women in "scant but gaudy uniforms" performed before rowdy male spectators and were in intimate contact with male coaches, trainers and masseurs.[27] In 1924, the Women's Division of the National Amateur Athletic Federation (U.S.A.) recommended that women coach girls' and women's teams. Clearly, these concerns were related to the possibility of sexual impropriety and exploitation. Apparently, the young athletes were not lacking in heterosexual appeal; they seemed to be blessed with an excess of it!

Many of the other concerns of the Women's Division were well-founded. A long-standing problem that escalated around this time was the tendency for spectators and journalists to show greater interest in "the scantily draped feminine form than in feminine athletic prowess."[28] Although such undisguised preoccupation was obviously exploitative of women, the Women's Division's stand against all competition failed to address the underlying issues of objectification and male power.

Few of the journalists who showed an interest in women's athletic prowess could resist the temptation to compare male and female performances, even though blatant inequality of opportunity in sport made such comparisons unfair and demoralizing. Discussing the "glorified tomboys" of the American women's Olympic track and field team, one male journalist compared men's and women's records to show the extent of female "physical inferiority."[29] Having established that women posed no serious threat to men, given the unquestioned male standard of excellence and the historical development of sports best suited to male physique and ability, men could afford to be cavalier or charitable about women's achievement. Another journalist expressed admiration for a golfer whose game was "masculine in its firm delicacy of touch"; he declared that she played good golf "even for a man [sic]."[30]

The Women's Division's recommendation that women's sport be controlled by women represented, in part, an attempt to avoid the competitiveness, commercialization and elitism seen to be inseparable from the male competitive model. In this respect, it was potentially a progressive movement that allowed for the autonomous development of women's sport, independent of media hyperbole and the "star" mentality.

The term "tomboy" is becoming obsolete, not because of the disappearance of the type but because it is accepted as normal. The danger is rather that athletics for women will get the wrong kind of advertising from the Olympic Games and that a new portent, the athletic star, will effectually discourage general participation in games by calling attention to the few who can win championships.

Blanche Trilling,
"The Playtime of a Million Girls
or an Olympic Victory — Which?"
in *Women and Athletics* edited by Women's
Division, National Amateur Athletic
Federation (New York: Barnes, 1930), p. 82

Yet the lobby against competition was suppported by conservative arguments (invariably invoking patriarchal definitions of femininity and motherhood) especially when there was a medical rationale, or even medical speculation, that the activity was unsafe for girls and women. The Women's Section of the American Physical Education Association, for example, condemned "formal spectator athletic contests in any activity for women because of their effect on health and character."[31]

Women in sports leadership positions were no doubt aware that male tolerance for women's sport depended on clearcut sex differentiation in the sports played, the extent and nature of participation, and the appearance and behaviour of the players. Around the turn of the century, there had been little to suggest that women's performance would ever approach men's, or that women were capable of participating in the full range of sporting activities and competitive levels. There was limited opportunity for competition outside schools and universities, the number of participants and the range of sports were small, and the few talented female athletes who gained public recognition could be treated as exceptions or anomalies.

Following the war, however, there were marked changes in female participation rates and performance. The narrowing of the gap between men's and women's records in swimming and track and field, first documented in the late 1920s, supported the argument that male supremacy was an "illusion."[32] Furthermore, girls and women were showing increasing interest and competence in team sports such as basketball, softball, ice hockey and lacrosse. Opportunities for intercollegiate, regional and national competition in these areas first opened up in the 1920s and early 1930s; there were, as well, some international events involving Canada, the U.S.A. and England. However, it was not until 1964 that a team sport for women — volleyball — was introduced into Olympic competition.

These developments clearly challenged the illusion of male supremacy. It was no longer legitimate to argue that all males were physically superior to all females, or that men had innate leanings towards competitive team sports while women were content with individual recreational pursuits. Thus, it is not surprising that there was widespread support from conservative sectors within education, the recreation movement and the church for the Women's Division recommendations. This resulted in the phasing out of interschool and intercollegiate competition for girls and young women throughout most American states and in some parts of Canada by the early 1930s.

♦

Track and field meet, Toronto Board of Education, undated. Women like this sprinter were breaking the traditional feminine stereotype.

CHAPTER FOUR

THE EVOLUTION OF HETEROSEXUALITY

BY THE 1930s, sex and marriage manuals popularized Freudian psychology and brought an end to the "age of innocence" regarding close relationships between women. Explained as manifestations of retarded sexual development, they were successfully pathologized by moralists of the day. Earlier isolated allegations of lesbianism directed at feminists and sportswomen had lacked the legitimation of Freudian psychology, which stigmatized same-sex relationships and other behaviours termed "sex-role non-conformity."[1]

An important function of the prescriptive literature was to promote the ideal of companionate marriage, based on friendship and mutual sexual gratification rather than on the traditional hierarchical relationship.[2] One of the few positive aspects of the latter, however, had been its acceptance of female friendship. The concept of companionate marriage promoted competition rather than solidarity among women, rendering a husband a more valued prize because, in his new role as companion, he was to satisfy all of a woman's social, emotional and sexual needs. Co-education, early dating and marriage, and the discouraging of close same-sex friendships were aimed at socializing young women (and men) towards the "heterosexual goal" (marriage).[3] The use of the term "heterosexual" is significant: in the literature of an earlier period, "sexual" implied "heterosexual."

Freudian psychology was not the only factor in promoting and controlling heterosexual activity among youth. Wartime loss of life, low birthrates, high infant mortality, and a high female mortality rate due to tuberculosis contributed to the emphasis on marriage and motherhood in the postwar years. As social and economic conditions changed, the expansion of women's sphere and the subsequent blurring of sex roles were further causes for concern.

Following the relatively liberal 1920s, the Depression of the 1930s was accompanied by a general shift back to the conservative values that contemporary social analyses tended to reflect and reinforce. On the question of sex differentiation and lesbianism, for example, one psychologist claimed that "economic and social forces" strengthened homosexual tendencies: "the boyish figure, skill in athletics, executive ability, success in business or professional life, enable the woman to approximate the conventional masculine ideal ... in many physical and mental characteristics."[4]

Although 1920s trends had not been entirely conducive to the "heterosexual goal," the flapper figure and fashions were, in fact, "boyish" rather than "mannish." Like many subsequent fashion fads, this style infantilized rather than masculinized women. Admittedly, there has long been a fine balance between crossdressing for fashion and cross-dressing as a symbol of "male identification." However, wearing of men's clothes was likely to be suspect if the wearer failed to satisfy other current standards of beauty or femininity.

More serious was the equating of any sign of athletic or intellectual competence with masculinity, and, by extension, with lesbianism. One journalist claimed that men often found competent women unappealing. Presumably they lacked the feminine traits of emotionalism, passivity and helplessness that validated masculine identity.

Whatever the rationale, successful women, whether in business or sport, were in a no-win situation. Although their performance was measured against male standards, other aspects of their behaviour and personality were judged according to the feminine ideal. If they were found wanting, the burden of proof to establish their heterosexual identity rested with them. Thus, the unathletic or unintelligent woman suffered no handicap in men's estimation as long as she was attractive. Although beauty redeemed a lack of intellectual ability, the reverse was not true. Moreover, it seemed that athletic ability did not redeem any feminine inadequacies. Beating a man at golf was hardly conducive to a harmonious relationship.[5]

> ... women who have ability in several directions have a certain masculinity in their attitude towards life which sets up a barrier between men and them ...It is difficult to think that a woman who can think clearly, who has executive ability, who has an understanding of the arts, who can be a leader in social life and in sports...should have anything but a man's broad outlook on life in general.
>
> ... as long as men are men will they want to worship rather than admire, and as long as women are women will they want to be worshipped rather than admired.
>
> Mona Clark,
"Are Brains a Handicap to a Woman?"
Canadian Magazine (February 1928): 27.

Some well-meaning male journalists interviewed female athletes, sportswriters and medical experts to prove that female athletes had lost none of their femininity. The women were portrayed as having a consuming interest in the clothes, grooming and hairstyles that heterosexual attractiveness required. These women were not "shy or diffident," nor were they "rough or repellent"; rather, their behaviour was "sweet and ladylike."[6] A more scholarly investigation reported no striking personality differences between athletic and non-athletic girls. In fact, the study identified nine "desirable" traits, including "beautiful or pretty," that were positively correlated to athleticism.[7]

Alexandrine Gibb, women's track coach and sports columnist, assured readers that the female athlete of the 1930s was not like her Victorian counterpart: "The masculine girl was an oddity of the Victorian age. Nowadays, a girl, essentially feminine, does not become masculine because she sprints or plays softball."[8] These enlightened sportswriters of the 1930s blamed sceptical journalists and critics at the turn of the century for popularizing the image of the female athlete as a "strident, belligerent Amazon."[9] The early sportswoman had been characterized as "a mannish creature ... she wore tweeds, took long, manly strides and spoke in a deep voice."[10]

Yet the apologetic approach of the 1930s also had its shortcomings. It was primarily through newly popularized associations between "masculine" women and lesbianism that sexual innuendos concerning these early athletes could be legitimized. The 1930s apologists failed to acknowledge that nineteenth-century sportswomen had paved the way for later generations of female athletes. Their stigmatization of these pioneers contributed to the historical invisibility of women in sport.

The little stone fragment of the goddess of sport from the ruins of ancient Crete, 16 centuries B.C., shows by comparison with the modern goddess of sport that there has been a decided improvement in the art of Corsetry.

Helen's
House of Corsetry

Sport ENHANCES Woman-hood

The little stone fragment of the goddess of sport from the ruins of ancient Crete, 16 centuries B.C., shows by comparison with the modern goddess of sport that there has been a decided improvement.

Compare the illustration from Frederick Griffin's article, "Sport Enhances Womanhood," Toronto Star Weekly (October 10, 1931), p.16, with the corset advertisement (on the left) that appeared the next week (October 17), p.4.

By the late 1930s, the question of the day was: were female athletes attractive to men? Muscles, strength, strain, sweat and dirt were offensive and unfeminine, according to one male journalist: "What male does not want girls to be sweetly feminine, and nice and sweet and frilly?" He characterized one sprinter, dubbed the "Galloping Ace," as "a big, lanky, flat-chested girl with as much sex appeal as grandmother's old sewing machine." Attributing her success to her "masculinity," he concluded that "beauty and success in girls' track and field sports don't go together so well."[11]

Responding to this tirade, champion hurdler Roxy Atkins, whom sportswriters had judged "the most beautiful competitor" in the Los Angeles Olympics, called for girls and women to have an equal chance as men to share in the benefits, material and social, of unrestricted sporting participation. She challenged the "masculine" label, emphasizing that "innuendoes" concerning the "Galloping Ace" were false, and citing numerous examples of sportswomen who were attractive, feminine and "gilt-edged securities in the marriage market."[12]

As for sweat and dirt, Atkins asked, "Would [men] have us run races with a powder puff in one hand and a mirror in the other?" Her question proved prophetic: one year later, a photo-story on the Women's National Swimming Championships in *Life* included two photographs of a swimmer combing her hair and putting on lipstick, with a mirror in one hand. She was also shown posed in a racing start, but none of the eleven photographs showed a swimmer in the water.[13] More than twenty years later, in 1960, a young woman participating in a high school charity football game was photographed taking a "powder break" just as Atkins had described.[14]

Some publications in the 1930s reported women's sport in much the same way as men's, providing facts and figures and including action photographs rather than the posed "feminine athlete" variety. These ranged from traditional activities like tennis, golf and swimming, and others, such as polo and track and field, in which women's participation had only a short history.[15]

The New York weekly, *The Literary Digest*, published one of the first practical articles on women's self-defence in North America.

"Training the Helpless Flapper to Fight Her Own Battles," which appeared in 1927, included an interview with jiu jitsu instructor Captain O'Brien, who described the techniques that women could use in dangerous situations. The article noted that "new and menacing conditions introduced by the automobile and other modern factors" made women more vulnerable to attacks by men. Illustrations showed a woman overpowering a well-dressed male attacker (Captain O'Brien).[16]

It is probably not surprising that jiu jitsu, a Japanese martial art introduced into England by H. Irving Hancock around 1900, was slow to cross the Atlantic. Hancock's book was reviewed in a New York periodical in 1904, but there was no suggestion that American women should emulate Japanese women, one of whom had won four out of five sparring bouts against Hancock.[17] By 1910, however, British suffragists were putting their jiu jitsu training to good effect to resist arrest. Photographs in a London newspaper showed their instructor, Mrs. Garrud, demonstrating her expertise on a policeman.[18] These events graphically dramatized the primary reason for male opposition to women in combat sports — fear that the imbalance of physical power between the sexes would be corrected. It was not until the 1970s and 1980s, however, that these issues became controversial.

Many journalists showed a preoccupation with finding classical figures with whom to identify sportswomen, Amazon being a favourite with both detractors and supporters.[19] More creative allusions, used in a positive manner, included "husky daughters of Athene and Artemis," "modern Atalantas" and "modern Dianas," choices intended to demonstrate that athletic ability was not incompatible with femininity.[20] Amazon, however, denoted both warrior and athlete, and thus lent itself to positive and negative allusions. There was virtually no equivalent term for males in sport, although circus strongmen were often named Atlas or Samson, perhaps for a similar reason: to dramatize the fact that they were different from ordinary mortals, perhaps freakish.

This need to emphasize the femininity of sportswomen stemmed from the anomaly that they posed. Despite their obvious progress in athletic performance, women's inherent and immutable physical inferiority remained axiomatic. If, indeed, these were "real" women, as the evidence — Roxy Atkins, in particular — seemed to suggest, journalists apparently felt constrained to remind readers of this fact. Yet, they were just as ready to point out the incongruities. For example, in an otherwise objective report on women in the 1936 Olympics, American sprinter Helen Stephens, "the fastest woman in the world" was also described as "the bobbed-haired, flat-chested, boyishly built runner." Somewhat surprisingly, there were no references to the appearance of her rival, Stella Walsh, who was probably the "Galloping Ace."[21]

ONLY FOR THE WAR'S DURATION

The suspension of Olympic and other international competition during the Second World War stalled the development of women's sport in several areas. But team sports such as basketball and softball had industrial sponsors and continued to thrive as women took up work in munitions and aircraft factories. Gladys Ross started work at a small arms factory in Toronto in 1943. Shortly thereafter, she was "recruited" by Vickers Aircraft, solely because of her reputation as a softball player.[22]

Women in the armed forces, too, were able to participate in softball and basketball leagues, track and field meets and rifle shooting contests. Recreational tennis, swimming, badminton and volleyball were also offered, and their practical training, of course, included marching drill and calisthenics. In 1943, female students at the University of New Hampshire became the first American women to undergo pre-graduation training similar to men's Reserve Officers' Training Corps, to equip them for service in the armed forces. A *Life* photograph showed young women, wearing shorts, marching through the snow and completing a commando-style training course. The article noted, however, that the program was suspended for a few days before the Military Art Ball because "the girls were too stiff to dance."[23]

Wartime conditions raised public awareness that women were vulnerable to sexual and other kinds of assault. Their war work often required traveling at late hours, in dimmed-out streets and in unsafe areas. The war also increased general lawlessness, according to Major Fairbairn, the author of a 1942 *New York Times* article that provided step-by-step instruction in women's self-defence. Fairbairn's system was based on commando-training methods in the British Army which incorporated judo techniques as well as defences with a walking stick or an umbrella.[24]

In 1943, American chewing-gum millionaire Philip Wrigley established a women's professional softball league to entertain

Combining exercise and corsetry, in an advertisement from Echoes *(Christmas 1943), p.24.*

workers in factory towns around Chicago after the military draft had decimated the American and National Baseball Leagues. In existing semi-professional women's teams, with names like Slapsy Maxie's Curvaceous Cuties and Num Num Pretzel Girls, "masculine" appearance and "hoydenish antics" (like swearing at the umpire) were tolerated. But Wrigley set out to clean up the game.[25] He took a paternal interest in players, enforcing a strict dress code and "ladylike" behaviour through a system of monetary fines. Slacks or "skin-tight" shorts, "masculine hair-cuts and tomboy styling," public drinking and smoking were forbidden. The specially designed skirt worn by Wrigley's All-American Girls satisfied the demands of modesty as well as femininity: it was "as dignified as [a] field hockey costume ... [but] still had the provocativeness of a Sonya Henie skating skirt." Wrigley screened prospective league members and rejected several "outstanding" players on the grounds that they were "too uncouth, too hard-boiled or too masculine."[26] His training program included a compulsory course in makeup and posture.

It is not difficult to understand Wrigley's business strategy, since his name and his product were closely associated with b..seball. If women's baseball was to replace men's for the duration, spectators must be won over, and feminine allure was a more saleable commodity than the skill of the players. Female softball players already had a reputation as "hoydens" and "tomboys" in some quarters, so Wrigley selected and rewarded women with heterosexual appeal. No doubt, there were some excellent softball players among the All-Americans, but there was no room for non-conformity, regardless of ability.

Wrigley also represented the ideological conservatism common in periods of social change. Perceiving developments in women's softball as aping the worst characteristics of male players, he advocated a return to traditional feminine values. His control and exploitation differed only slightly from other industrial sponsors who profited from players' heterosexual appeal. More than twenty years later, the promoters of girls' rules basketball in Iowa operated on similar principles.

The female athletes of the 1930s and 1940s escaped public criticism for their unconventional preoccupation with sport only when they paid the prerequisite attention to the feminine image. Success in sport was assumed to be incompatible with femininity or heterosexuality; hence, the sexual identities of growing numbers of women were suspect. In a society where conformity to the heterosexual norm was rewarded with visible power and privilege, the barriers to sportswomen were formidable.

THE SPORTSWOMAN
AND THE FEMININE MYSTIQUE

Postwar conservatism has been described by Betty Friedan: women should desire "no greater destiny than to glory in their own femininity." Careers or commitments outside the home were unnecessary for their personal fulfilment and undesirable for the satisfactory performance of the housewife role.[27] Women's wartime gains in employment soon disappeared. They were laid off non-traditional jobs as men returned home to resume their rightful place. The All-American Girls eventually suffered the same fate.

In women's education, the heterosexual goal was increasingly emphasized. "Preparation for the problems of marriage" was a crucial function of women's college education. Psychology and home economics courses instructed women in interpersonal relations and household management skills. These were, apparently, the sole responsibility of the woman.[28] Other educators proposed that this process start well before college, stressing the need for recreation programs that helped "little girls grow up to become better mothers, better homemakers, better leaders of their families of the future."[29] The more liberal attitudes and practices of the 1920s and 1930s were long gone.

In the 1940s and 1950s, the usual postwar premium on human resources — the wealth of the nation — took the form of renewed government concern for the health and recreational needs of citizens. In Canada, the various provincial and national fitness and recreation programs established during the war reflected the traditional practice of providing team sports for males and fitness activities for females. A New York program offered women calisthenics and ball games in addition to lectures on baseball, football and boxing, in order to further their "understanding of American sports"; in other words, to equip them for the female role of spectator and supporter.[30]

This role was institutionalized in the increasing prominence of cheerleaders in the postwar period. Although some American universities had cheerleaders by the turn of the century, most were male, partly because the task of leading the cheers was well suited to the deeper male voice. Their performance also included jumps, kicks and somersaults, and, by about 1930, some American coaches were permitting female cheerleaders because of their "better sense of rhythm."[31] By the 1940s, the decorative function had clearly become as important as gymnastic and cheering ability. One newspaper photograph of cheerleaders at a high school football final was headed "Inspiration for any halfback"; the caption read, "This is what helps any halfback to risk his neck for another yard of ground."[32] Women's vicarious involvement in sport was best symbolized in the classic and cliché shot of a cheerleader holding the winning team's trophy.[33]

Cheerleaders and beauty queens (and an occasional typing contest winner) were virtually the only female high school students featured in local newspapers. School yearbooks showed a similar neglect of girls' sport.[34] Not surprisingly, girls learned their proper place at an early age.

A whole new world opened up for me [in grade 10] i.e. sports, and athletic boys! We were great followers of all the activities during and after school, and Jean even talked me into trying out for a cheerleader and class rep.

Velma Davis's memoirs,
Northern Secondary School
1950s Scrapbook.

The assumptions regarding sport, femininity and hetero-sexuality were rarely questioned by physical educators. Elizabeth Halsey, a university physical educator writing in 1961, devoted considerable space to the "unfavourable stereotype" of female physical education majors, reinforced by those who failed to pay sufficient attention to clothing, grooming and deportment. Every major had a responsibility "to make the most of her looks" in order to correct prevailing misconceptions. One of her recommendations for helping the "tomboys" to arrive at "a better attitude" was "to publicise the most charming looking students" through the election of baseball queens, field hockey queens and archery queens whose portraits, "*not* in sports clothes," were prominently displayed.[35]

At some universities, however, more dramatic steps were taken to deal with the "undesirable stereotype." In the 1960s, Rita Mae Brown, as a student whose lesbianism was known, was threatened by female physical education students who warned her not to associate with any of their number, presumably because of a fear of guilt by association.[36] Similar reasoning probably prompted a female physical educator to screen out prospective physical education majors if they were "masculine" types.[37]

Participation in school, university and community sporting programs, however, was hardly likely to pose a threat to femininity. Basketball continued, for the most part, to be played by girls' rules. As late as 1952, its proponents were citing "expert" physiological and psychological rationales for the less demanding game.[38] Softball, an already simplified version of baseball, was in some cases modified further for girls and women — there was a "no sliding" rule, for example.[39] Track events were restricted to distances as short as 100 yards, even though by 1960 the 800 metres race had been reinstated in Olympic competition.[40]

It is not surprising that some girls tried, with varying success, to gain admission to boys' teams. A 1955 *Life* story told how a "pretty farm girl" turned out to be the star of the boys' baseball team.[41] Around the same time, future Canadian Olympic runner Abby Hoffman gained admission to a boys' hockey team in Toronto because she was registered as A. Hoffman and looked like a boy. Her expertise, no doubt, made the strategy a success.[42]

That these girls' experiences were publicized was, of course, a potentially positive force in encouraging others to follow.

However, for girls whose ability was less than exceptional, there were far greater obstacles to overcome. As in many other areas of endeavour, higher than male standards were applied to girls and women, and astonishment expressed when they met these standards. Personal appearance was clearly a factor; the femininity quotient of the girl in question served to underline the rare "beauty and brawn" combination. In Hoffman's case, looking like a boy helped in the sporting context, if not elsewhere in the era of the feminine mystique.

THEY DON'T LOOK LIKE WOMEN

From the time of the 1952 Olympic games, when the U.S.S.R. participated for the first time, journalists discovered a new "Amazon"— the Soviet sportswoman. A 1952 article referred to the "hand-picked Russian Amazons" who would confront the American track and field team. The American women would be forgiven, it was implied, if they did not surpass the Amazons' performances.[43] The overwhelming success of Soviet women in track and field events and the Cold War mentality of the 1950s and 1960s contributed to this unflattering portrayal in the media. The results of Olympic competition in volleyball, the first women's team sport in the Olympics, reinforced these stereotypical distinctions: Japan and the U.S.S.R. won the gold medals throughout the 1960s and 1970s. While not Amazons in physique, the Japanese volleyball players, who worked and trained in an Osaka factory, were as un-American and unfeminine as their Soviet counterparts. One Japanese player was quoted as saying that, while the tough training regimen exacted a price in terms of social life, injuries, and limbs that were not "as gracefully shaped as those of our sisters," the most important consideration was "the pride of bringing some sporting glory to the company and our nation."[44] Admittedly, these were not typical Japanese women, but their North American counterparts were unlikely even to be mentioned in the media if their sporting involvement devalued their worth on the marriage market. Moreover, for many North Americans, female athletes' loyalty to a team or company was an alien concept.

With these "unfeminine" women out-performing western athletes, doctors and sports administrators developed an interest in biological as well as social definitions of femininity. Both ideological and nationalistic motives were at work. Clearly, sexual ambiguity, whether clinical or social, posed a threat to compulsory heterosexuality and male dominance. It is ironic, therefore, that subsequent developments in genetics and endocrinology reduced biological femininity to the single criterion of chromosomal count, while rendering the social and ethical questions increasingly complex.[45]

Official rationales for sex tests make reference to the unfairness of contests between women and individuals who are not female, yet there is the inherent suggestion that athletic achievement is not a characteristic of "real women." Therefore the sexual identity of successful female athletes is automatically suspect. Such suspicions and fears crystallized around four or five known cases in a fifty-year period of female participation in international sport. The result was a battery of imperfect, but impressive, official procedures.

Eligibility to participate in women's international sporting events had been decided on the basis of a medical certificate from the athlete's home country. In 1955 it was revealed that a man had won the Olympic women's high jump for Germany in the 1936 Olympics; he claimed he had been forced to pose as a woman. Three medal winners at the 1946 European Athletic Championships subsequently declared themselves to be men. These were cases of male pseudo-hermaphroditism: having "male-like genitals and physique, or unusual growth of hair on the face" as well as chromosomal or hormonal indicators of maleness. The argument was that they should have been disqualified from female competition on the grounds that their strength was abnormal for a woman.[46]

At the 1966 European Championships in Budapest, the first official "sex tests" were introduced, with three female gynecologists conducting visual examinations to confirm that athletes' external genital sex was, in fact, female. The venue and timing were significant. The U.S.S.R. was represented in large numbers, and it had been the track and field athletes —especially the Soviet women — who had attracted considerable public attention and conjecture during the preceding decade. At the 1967 Championships, screening became more rigorous as chromosomal testing was added to the visual test.

In considering the implications of these sex tests, it is important to note that chromosomal anomalies are not necessarily indicative of masculinity. Most women with an extra X chromosome, for example, are not different from other women in terms of physical and muscular development, and do not have an unfair advantage in sporting contests. That this particular sex test may fail to determine ineligibility was argued in medical circles as early as 1968.[47] More recently, Australian researcher Kenneth Dyer pointed to the remarkable improvements in women's performance since the introduction of the test; clearly, it was not just the chromosomally different athletes who were breaking the records.[48]

However, the inadequacies of this sex test were rarely considered by sports admininstrators in the 1960s and 1970s. Even many of the female athletes involved were reported to have approved the rationale behind it: one expressed concerns about competitors with "5 o'clock shadows."[49] With public attention directed at their sexual identity, it is probably not surprising that some athletes made a deliberate and concerted effort to establish a feminine, heterosexual identity. Even as talented an athlete as Babe Didrikson reportedly said, "I know I'm not pretty, but I try to be graceful." Another successful track athlete, Fanny Blankers-Koen of the Netherlands, was equally realistic about public acclaim: "People applaud me because I do my training and winning between washing dishes and darning socks."[50]

Rumours and innuendos circulated by the press at the time of the first sex test made it clear that certain athletes were considered guilty of "masculinity" until proven innocent. Following the Budapest events, two athletes who had refused the test on ethical or religious grounds, and three Soviet women who did not participate for various reasons, were suspected of sexual abnormality. The point was driven home in the press: pictures showing the straining face of Soviet hurdler Irina Press were juxtaposed with the "demure and motherly" Mary Rand, smiling and holding her young daughter.[51]

According to one athlete, the doctors responsible for the testing scrutinized flat-chested women with particular insensitivity.[52] Following the 1968 Olympics, the chief sex tester, Ludwig Prokop, told reporters that his examination of 911 female athletes had convinced him that sports made them ugly, with hard, stringy bodies and, in some cases, hair on their chests.[53] Muscularity in athletes was hardly a cause for comment, and one study showed that 17 percent of women had hair growth around their nipples.[54]

The good doctor's preoccupation with chests is illuminating, as the external genitals were ostensibly the focus of the visual examination. More importantly, Prokop and his colleagues, charged with the responsibility of evaluating biological femaleness, obviously had difficulty distinguishing it from beauty or sex appeal. Another male expert on flat-chestedness, the coach of the University of Pennsylvania women's rowing team, claimed that "constant use of the pectoral muscles flattens the bosom," while maintaining that "a lean oarsman [sic] is an attractive woman."[55]

Polish-American track and field athlete, Stella Walsh, participated in Olympic competition in the 1930s and 1940s, before mandatory sex testing. Although comments on her masculine appearance were not unusual, it was not until after her death in 1981 that it was discovered that she had male-like genitals. There is little doubt, however, that North American journalists were kinder to Walsh during her lifetime than to masculine athletes from the U.S.S.R. Irina and Tamara Press, for example, known to sportswriters as the "Press Brothers," were described as "squat troglodytes with short haircuts and enormous thighs."[56]

By the late 1960s, a new focus of concern was the use of anabolic steroids by female athletes. As early as the 1930s there had been evidence that muscular hypertrophy could be induced in mammals of both sexes by androgenic hormones; their use by male athletes was well documented by the early 1970s.[57] In 1968, steroid use by Olympic competitors was ruled illegal, but it was not until 1976 that the International Amateur Athletic Federation introduced random spot testing at international competitions.

While there are equally valid ethical reasons for disqualifying both male and female steroid users, female offenders, whose sexual identity is perceived as encroaching on men's, have frequently been subjected to particularly vicious ridicule and censure. The intake of synthetic hormones may reduce a male user's hormone production, with resultant loss of libido, decrease in testicular size and lowered sperm count. But these changes tend to be overshadowed by the highly visible and undeniably masculine increases in weight, muscle mass and strength. For women, however, the side effects are socially as well as ethically undesirable: some female steroid users exhibit external signs of "virilization," which attract as much attention as the ethical implications and the health concerns.[58]

Virilization describes the physiological changes which may be experienced by female steroid users: deepening of the voice, increased facial and body hair, changes in libido, clitoral enlargement, diminished breast mass and menstrual irregularities. Many of the same indicators are to be found in individuals with choromosomal abnormalities; the sex test would confirm this condition.[59] Not coincidentally, some of the same features have long been associated with the "masculine" lesbian, a stereotype supported by hormonal theories of lesbianism.[60]

Clearly, it is not valid to make allegations of steroid use of chromosomal abnormality (or lesbianism) based on one or more signs of virilization, as these symptoms have numerous other physiological causes. Thus, the introduction of sex and drug testing failed to alleviate the problems of the female athlete. A woman with one or more of these indicators associated with ambiguous sexual identity and sexual orientation as well as steroid use was triply suspect, even though a single indicator — flat-chestedness or a deep voice, for example — was not a reliable predictor of chromosomal anomaly or steroid use (and had no bearing, of course, on lesbianism). Distance runners, for example, are typically flat-chested and amenorrheic, but it has been among female track and field athletes that most steroid users and hermaphrodites have been detected.

East German female swimmers at the 1976 Olympics were among the first to be suspected of steroid use. Again, nationalistic

*T*rack and field meet, Toronto Board of Education, undated.

fervour and East-West rivalry muddied the issues, as did the pervasive assumption that femininity and heterosexuality were incompatible with athletic excellence. American athletes' comments on the "huge" muscular physique of the East German women who won eleven out of fourteen swimming events ranged from grudging admiration of their weight training program to allegations of steroid use. It was obvious that the East Germans were being evaluated on aesthetic rather than athletic standards of performance. Some of the American women were quoted as saying that they certainly did not want to look like the East Germans, whatever the cost in medals; after all, "they don't look exactly like they're girls."[61]

Attempts to explain "cultural differences" made matters worse: "East German women say they are happy the way they are ... and East Germany's national sport commitment makes lifting weights more important than wearing makeup." American swimmers' alleged dislike of weight training was justified on the grounds that "the physiological and psychological effect of seeing themselves with broader shoulders would create further complications in a social life already inhibited by rigid practice schedules." More simply, broad shoulders would make them feel unattractive to men or would detract from their sex appeal. Even the fact that East German gold medallist Kornelia Ender was engaged to a member of the men's swimming team did not establish her femininity. American swimmers reportedly viewed the relationship as "a genetic extension of East Germany's superman sport concept."[62]

Whether the allegations of steroid use were valid is not the major issue — athletes of both sexes from western and eastern bloc countries have been disqualified since testing was instituted. Other factors were at work: in particular, a narrow definition of femininity. As one isolated supporter asserted, East German women "are capable of viewing themselves as attractive, sexual women, not by their measurements, but because of who they are as human beings."[63] Such reasoning was of little consolation to sportswomen who failed the social, if not the biological, femininity test. Women's track and field coach Pat Connelly voiced a common view: steroid use made "freaks out of women. Women are beautiful creatures the way God made them ... By taking a male hormone, a woman is really changing what she is all about."[64]

There is little to suggest that attitudes and practices have changed. At the First World Championships of Track and Field in 1983, Czech Jarmila Kratochvilova was the target of similar attacks, alleging that "there will always be doubt about her femininity." Mary Decker, an American runner, reportedly refused to refer to Eastern bloc athletes as "she," using instead the word "person."[65] An American hurdler noted that, the preceding year, Kratochvilova "had breasts"; now she has "a very flat, muscular chest."[66]

Before sophisticated steroid testing came into effect in 1984, both male and female athletes commonly avoided detection by stopping steroid intake a few days before the test, leading at least one doctor to question why any steroid user was ever caught.[67] However, what is relevant is the implication that female steroid users commit a crime against nature, whereas male users are merely misguided or misinformed. If the balance of so-called male and female hormones is seen as crucial, then male users are equally guilty of tampering with nature and their sexual identity.

The feminine mystique of the 1950s and 1960s further entrenched the incompatibility between sporting achievement and femininity. The suspect components of the sportswoman's identity — physical, psychological and sexual — were increasingly subject to public scrutiny and innuendo. Procedures designed to bring about fair sporting competition among women only added to the stigmatization of the female athlete. By the 1970s, however, as the feminist and lesbian/gay rights movements gained support, women were successfully challenging sexism and heterosexism in sport.

♦

$\mathbf{B}$asketball, *Toronto Board of Education, undated.*

CHAPTER FIVE

THE SEXUALITY ISSUE

THROUGHOUT THE CENTURY of women's mass sporting participation, femininity and heterosexuality have been seen as
incompatible with sporting excellence: either sport made women
masculine, or sportswomen were masculine at the outset. In the
last half-century, the term "masculine" has often implied lesbian.
Such reasoning reinforced the polarized view of masculinity and
femininity, both social and biological, thereby underscoring sex
differences and legitimating male supremacy.

The polarity was illustrated in sport by chromosomal measures of sex phenotype and by two scholarly inventions: role
conflict among female athletes and the pathologizing of
"tomboyism." It is not coincidental that efforts to establish the
abnormal sex-role identity and sexual orientation of female
athletes were concurrent with a wave of feminism, nor is it new to
discredit female intruders in sport, politics, business and other
bastions of male supremacy as man-aping, man-hating and/or
lesbian.

During the 1970s, many experts addressed the alleged
problem of role conflict among female athletes; some remain
convinced that it exists.[1] Researchers investigated self-percep-
tions and the attitudes of peers, yet failed to examine the material
conditions surrounding female sporting participation. Few
considered the possibility that these conditions, rather than
nebulous "attitudes" or athletes' internal conflicts, might be the
major source of difficulties.

Such studies labelled sporting activities as masculine and feminine, hypothesizing that female participation in traditionally male sports was associated with lower peer acceptance and greater role conflict. Related investigations of the sex-role orientation of female athletes hypothesized that psychological traits termed masculine (or, more recently, androgynous) predisposed girls and women to pursue certain sports.[2] Some early studies found positive associations, but it soon became clear that role conflict and masculine sex-role orientation among female athletes were by no means universal. Some persistent researchers, however, were committed either to normalizing female sporting participation, or to finding the elusive evidence to prove their hypothesis. Whatever the motive, the dichotomy between masculine and feminine sports and masculine and feminine sex-roles became entrenched, when the immediate issues for females in sport concerned equality of access to programs, facilities and funding.

This type of research had far-reaching implications for physical education, a profession already characterized by conservatism. For example, the alleged problem of "femininized" young men was seen as an outcome of women's liberation. Sport was correctly identified as a major factor in masculine identification; current trends promoting "the extended female role perception of certain sports and games" jeopardized this crucial process and should be challenged.[3] However, the cost to girls of keeping some sports exclusively male was apparently not worth calculating.

One physical educator listed nine "characteristic problems" in the area of gender identification, including preference for games of the opposite sex and passivity in male children; all were derived from environmental theories of homosexuality. He urged his colleagues to develop sex-differentiated sport and physical education programs, with remedial work for those children who exhibited "gender identification problems"; passive boys needed to be taught aggression through team games, while girls needed activities that discouraged competitiveness.[4]

> It is imperative that the masculine concepts of certain sports be retained ... Male children, both present and future, cannot afford to be deprived of yet another factor which influences masculine orientation.
>
> A. Craig Fisher,
> "Sports as an Agent
> of Masculine Orientation,"
> *Physical Educator*
> (October 1972): 120, 122.

> We must clearly identify the characteristics of childhood and adulthood which the American society values as being masculine or feminine ... We must teach our children ...through ... games and activities appropriate for proper sex-role identification.
>
> Peter Werner,
> "The Role of Physical Education
> in Gender Identification,"
> *Physical Educator* (March 1972): 28.

Theories of sex-role identification were closely related to research on female homosexuality. Terms such as "tomboy" and "Amazon" have had changing connotations since the turn of the century, but by the 1970s they were rarely complimentary. The childhood label "tomboy," for example, becomes the adult label "dyke."[5] From this context, sexologists developed a new approach to homosexuality. Childhood tomboyism, cross-gender wishes, alienation from peers and preference for boys' games became components of "Childhood Gender Nonconformity" and predictors of lesbianism in adult life.[6] Whereas environmental theories had tended to blame family background, gender nonconformity implied a propensity for lesbianism, manifested by tomboyish behaviour.

Lending some support to this explanation was a study of girls who had been exposed to excessive androgen prenatally, and had subsequently displayed more tomboyish behaviour than a control group. This led to the conclusion that "male hormones" accounted for these abnormalities: "tomboyism in fetally masculinized genetic females ... is a sequel to a masculinizing effect on the fetal brain."[7] This use of language legitimated a biodeterministic model, with its polarized, culturally and historically specific definitions of masculinity and femininity. The clinical term "tomboy" described girls who preferred activities, clothes and toys traditionally asociated with boys and termed "masculine" merely because of contemporary North American convention.[8]

The argument fitted well with the new theories of homosexuality: if tomboyism was a predictor of lesbianism, and if tomboyism was the result of male/female hormonal imbalance, ergo lesbianism had a hormonal and/or innate basis. One study warned that tomboyism was not as "innocuous" as commonly believed: 70 percent of a sample group of lesbians had been tomboys, compared to 16 percent in the general population.[9] It was difficult, however, to explain the 16 percent figure, more than five times the author's estimated rate of lesbianism. Moreover, a later study showed that from 51 percent to 78 percent of all women considered themselves to have been tomboys, as did a clear majority of successful women in politics, law, business and the arts, as well as sport.[10] Two explanations are possible: that the association between tomboyism and lesbianism is tenuous, or that the socializing effects of compulsory heterosexuality are more pervasive and powerful than commonly assumed, restricting the options for many women who might otherwise choose lesbianism. The term "tomboy" is clearly an inadequate scientific measure of behaviour; yet, by the 1970s, it had become the mainstay of research on gender nonconformity and lesbianism, as sexologists began with the stereotype of the masculine lesbian and worked backwards.[11]

The pathologizing of the play patterns of so-called tomboys parallels Freudian theories of penis envy, which feminist critics have explained as a well-founded envy for the superior status that males enjoy, apparently on account of this biological difference.[12] The girl who prefers boys' company and boys' games may be equally pragmatic. The boys enjoy greater freedom and independence while they play their "boys' games"; playing with dolls and tea-sets is hardly an apprenticeship in liberation.

The circular logic of this research turns between the poles of masculinity and femininity; girls should play feminine games, which are labelled feminine because girls traditionally played them. If they deviate from this pattern, their activities are not defined as feminine, because males have the powers of definition. Therefore, girls who pioneer new patterns are labelled masculine or deviant.

A study of women's softball showed that skills, game behaviours, appearance, uniforms, mannerisms, etc. displayed by female players were perceived as masculine because they were associated with male baseball players. Definitions of masculinity and femininity were clearly arbitrary. Masculine mannerisms included spitting, knocking dirt from shoes, whipping a ball around the infield, and walking in from positions to comfort the pitcher, none of which required biological attributes specific to males.[13] Thus, while the masculine style in sport is "the norm," it is not considered "normal" for girls and women to emulate it. In the familiar apologetic tone we are told that women accused of playing "like a man" are "not trying to copy men's movements," but "simply performing in the most effective way they can."[14]

> Coaches should put a damper on masculine mannerisms that are not necessary to a girl's performance or that create an undesirable impression ... [Such] mannerisms are frequently given as reasons for the public's negativism towards athletics for women ... The coach should seize every opportunity to improve the girl's behaviour. It may not make the woman a better athlete, but it will eventually make the athlete a better woman.
>
> Patsy Neal, *Coaching Methods for Women* (Reading, Massachusetts: Addison-Wesley, 1969), p. 106.

PRETTY PLAYERS
AND SEXY CHEERLEADERS

Girls' basketball coaches in Iowa were apparently still operating on the femininity principle in the late 1970s. One young player, defending the tradition of playing by girls' rules (now also called "split-court rules") explained, "Our coach says that the main reason we play basketball is to get poise and grace and become better ladies." The same coach permitted aggression on the court, but demanded a return to helplessness after the game, for "a lady is above opening doors for herself." Another coach asserted that the split-court game was "the prettiest thing about girls' basketball." The major promoter claimed that the game was amusing, not threatening to male patrons, who were further entertained by half-time shows starring provocatively dressed "girls."[15]

This is not to question basketball players' skill and dedication, or to assume that split-court rules necessarily made the game less challenging. In fact, Iowa basketball was constantly cited as a successful female spectator sport; and players did receive a level of public acclaim generally reserved for male athletes, "idolized in the media and the grandstands."[16] But there are other factors

C heerleaders, Toronto Board of Education, undated.

to consider. Although almost all of Iowa's high schools fielded girls' basketball teams and Iowa had the highest participation rate among school-age girls in the U.S.A., there were still marked inequities in budgets for boys' and girls' athletics. Moreover, basketball played by split-court rules was the subject of a 1979 Tennessee court decision. It was successfully argued that this rules restriction limited a high school girl's chances of winning a college athletic scholarship.[17]

Girls' rules basketball, with a tradition and ritual dating back to the 1920s, symbolized an unambiguous vision of women. There was no illusion that they were men's equal, no suggestion that they aspired to be like men, and no doubt as to their heterosexual orientation and appeal.

While girls' and women's participation in contact sports was only acceptable on these terms, women were welcomed unconditionally as spectators and cheerleaders for men's games. It has been proposed that the uniforms and routines of drum majorettes and drill teams symbolize sexuality subordinated to militarism.[18] Perhaps coaches' common practice of forbidding sexual activity prior to competition made the sight of provocative but inaccessible young female bodies produce even more sexual energy that could be channeled into the game.

Whatever the rationale, the presence of attractive, admiring women validates the display of masculinity and machismo on the playing field. Girls' apprenticeship for this role begins early in life. Schools and community centres routinely offer cheerleading instruction, and television reinforces the image of the sexy cheerleader. Ontario secondary schools listed cheerleading as a girls' "interschool athletic activity" as late as 1981-82. Admittedly, some schools allowed male cheerleaders, but integrated cheerleading was hardly a victory for sex equality advocates. In 1976, a Toronto Task Force on the Status of Women succeeded in removing cheerleading and baton-twirling from the so-called "physical recreation" activities offered to girls by the Parks and Recreation Department.[19]

It is significant that cheerleaders are associated primarily with the most brutal of men's team sports — football, for example — which have been described as "war without weapons."[20] In this analogy, cheerleaders, like the women in the stands, can be seen as camp followers. Of course, more creative rationales refer to team morale and fan support, and some women — the Toronto Argos cheerleaders, for example — see themselves in this role. The Argos coach, who apparently had final authority over cheerleaders as well as players, decided to replace their skimpy uniforms with more "orthodox" ones, and to restrict their association with players. This kind of paternalism was strongly resented by the women. However, it seemed that, had he required the skimpy uniforms or the social and sexual interaction with players that cheerleaders considered desirable (a lot of dating, according to one woman), his actions would not have been unpopular. Some cheerleaders had considered boycotting the game, but believed that they "owed it to the players."[21]

TELL THEM WE'RE AMAZONS

Athletes' sexual orientation became a topic of public discussion in 1981 when a lesbian relationship involving professional tennis champion Billie Jean King was the subject of legal proceedings. Some of the resulting media coverage attempted to address the broader issues rather than sensationalizing the specific case. Lesbianism in professional tennis and golf was explained primarily as a byproduct of the all-female setting, the loneliness of going on tour for more than half the year, and the problem of "country club lechers."[22]

A few years earlier, a golfer on the Ladies' Professional Golf Association tour expressed her discomfort at having "so many single women on the tour who are such good friends. I would like to see a Mrs. in front of each name."[23] Not coincidentally, 1977 had marked the beginning of Anita Bryant's anti-homosexual campaign, which injected new life into homophobic views of women's friendships.

A controversy developed in 1981 over the use of glamour photography to sell the golf tour; Jan Stephenson, "golf's reigning sex symbol," defended her participation by pointing out the necessity of beauty companies as sponsors. Indeed, one journalist observed that even "the most ardent gay activist" would probably keep her sexual preference private as long as

Players from a lesbian softball league, Toronto, 1984.

women's sport depended on commercial sponsors whose business it was to promote heterosexual glamour.[24]

It has been suggested that one factor in the alleged "high incidence" of lesbianism in sport was the tendency for many young heterosexual women to see themselves as cheerleaders, not participants.[25] Although simplistic, it is no doubt true that innuendos concerning lesbianism deterred some heterosexual athletes. That many lesbian athletes were alienated by homophobic attitudes and practices within sport received little media attention. Many female athletes still feel compelled to flaunt their heterosexual attractiveness; labels like "masculine" and "lesbian" retain their power to divide women, especially in sport.[26]

Athletes who took deliberate steps to cultivate a feminine public image conveyed a clear message. The apparent willingness of women like tennis player Chris Evert and golfer Nancy Lopez, for example, to have intimate details of their married lives revealed in magazines might also be interpreted in this way, although marketability was obviously an important factor. If female athletes were to be newsworthy, it was a good strategy for journalists to start with well-known women who conformed to the heterosexual norm, both in appearance and in lifestyle.[27] However, there have been several recent instances of heterosexual women in sport publicly expressing support for lesbian athletes.

Attempts were first made in the early 1970s to prove that fitness and muscle tone derived from sporting participation had a positive effect on female sexuality. Some men chose to call it "sexual performance"; in any case, they claimed that (heterosexual) female athletes were more active sex partners, had greater stamina and were uninhibited about their bodies. Men appeared more eager to prove this association than women, probably because they believed they would be the beneficiaries.[28]

Further "expert" advice on the enhancement of femininity through sport reassured women that their calf muscles would not become bulky through jogging. In fact, "by jogging in the right places," their "shapely calves" may even attract male attention.[29] When it became clear, however, that female joggers were a new target of sexual assault, the encouragement turned to criticism, as some males pronounced that female joggers who attracted male attention — by wearing shorts, for example — were "asking for it."[30]

In an alternative "sexy athlete" hypothesis, American pentathlete Jane Frederick listed the same characteristics as reasons for the incidence of lesbianism (or, in her own case, bisexuality) among athletes.[31] The 1982 film *Personal Best* supported Frederick's thesis in part, portraying a lesbian relationship between two pentathletes who were muscular, active and attractive women. While some critics objected to the standard heterosexual "happy ending," they acknowledged the strengths of the film, especially in making lesbians in sport visible and deemphasizing the stereotyped associations among tomboyism, masculinity and lesbianism.[32]

The publicity surrounding the King case had strengthened the institution of compulsory heterosexuality in the short term, yet it also marked the beginning of more open discussion on topics formerly cloaked in secrecy and innuendo. Developments in the feminist movement and the lesbian and gay rights movement were responsible for much of this change in attitude and practice, making it somewhat easier for athletes, whether lesbian or heterosexual, to confront these issues.

Although femininity and heterosexuality have long been central to women's sporting participation, it has only been in recent years that they have been discussed in relatively explicit terms. The salience of heterosexuality in the past decade can be explained in part as a heterosexist reaction to visible lesbians in sport and in society at large, just as the earlier emphasis on femininity was a sexist reaction to women who were competent — and visible — in sport, business or politics.

Two potential forums for debating this issue were provided in 1983 at the "New Agenda" conference (co-sponsored by the Women's Sport Foundation and the U.S. Olympic Committee in Washington) and at "A Renaissance in Sport and Fitness," a Toronto conference organized by the Ontario Women's Inter-university Athletic Association.

Both conferences succeeded in bringing female athletes together and focusing public and media attention on some of the political issues. But it does not appear that participants came close to resolving the femininity or heterosexuality issue. Although conference organizers did not view this as a central concern, a large number of presenters and participants raised the issue. Neither conference was, by design, feminist, although even an explicitly feminist organization, the Canadian Association for the Advancement of Women and Sport, encounters difficulties in dealing with this issue.[33]

In one of the few feminist presentations at the Toronto conference, Sport Canada director-general Abby Hoffman identified the ways in which ideology served to exclude women from sport. One of Hoffman's targets was the institutionalization of femininity of sportswomen, evident in the "cutesy-pie routines" of some gymnasts, figure skaters and synchronized swimmers, which are apparently intended to "mask their athleticism." As for television exercise shows, with their "obscene" portrayal of physically active women, Hoffman stated that it would be preferable to have "nothing."[34]

Hoffman's position was hardly shared by conference organizers, who reportedly intended it to be "a positive look at women in sports," not "an analysis of our problems."[35] The conference's goal, according to one journalist, was to seek alternatives to "the usual feminist approach" of "bitching and whining." The use of "sex appeal" to sell women's sports justified the end results: visibility and publicity. She dismissed the notion that the media might be expected to help change public attitudes; they were responsible only for reflecting the status quo.[36]

The proceedings of the New Agenda conference revealed a similar diversity on the political issues related to feminism and femininity. A resolution to support research and scholarship from a feminist perspective was voted down, because some participants correctly interpreted the word "feminist" to denote radicalism and militancy. Many of the participants, however, supported resolutions to have lesbianism discussed in a workshop and to help lesbians in homophobic situations. One feminist newspaper saw this apparent contradiction as a failure to see the political implications of lesbianism for women in sport; instead, it was being treated as an aspect of athletes' private lives for which they were subjected to unfair discrimination.[37]

Participants failed to make other connections between the personal and the political. Professional golfer Carol Mann, who rejected the feminist resolution, addressed the problem of social life and the female athlete. After her golfing career peaked, she had sought counseling in order to learn the kinds of feminine behaviours appropriate for dating and establishing relationships with men. A woman's commitment to excellence in sport, she claimed, meant "an isolation from the social norms." Her problems stemmed from the "masculine" traits of self-centredness, aggressiveness and determination that she had developed through golf; she had failed to develop the antithetical "feminine" traits needed to be acceptable to men.[38] Mann was not the first athlete to recognize the contradiction; yet she did not question the social system that gave males the power to define masculinity and femininity and to enforce the "social norms" that devalued women's sporting achievement.

> A woman must decide whether or not she can participate in competitive sports and, at the same time, enjoy satisfying and meaningful social relationships with men ... The male concept of what is properly and appropriately feminine is still a powerful role determinant.
>
> Diane de Bacy et al.,
> "What Do Men Really Think About Athletic Competition for Women?"
> *Journal of Health, Physical Education and Recreation*
> (November/December 1970): 28.

Entrenching the masculine/feminine dichotomy has had different, but equally important implications for lesbian athletes. By the 1980s, the issue was made increasingly visible in feminist publications, and, occasionally, in mainstream media. Visibility, however, had both positive and negative consequences: an article in *Coaching Review* warned Canadian athletes planning to accept American scholarships to avoid campuses where lesbianism among athletes was "a popular practice." Several readers objected to such blatant homophobia.[39]

Homophobia has created rifts between women in sport, as in the women's movement at large. Some athletes tolerated lesbians only until they began to seek visibility. Others, influenced by the "paranoia in sports circles," avoided playing on teams with lesbians.[40] It was not only heterosexual women who found lesbian visibility problematic. Many lesbians whose employment in sport-related jobs depended on concealing their lesbian identities also found it a problem. On a more positive note, some women formed lesbian-only outdoor clubs and sports leagues, while others developed organizations where lesbianism was accepted positively and sexual preference was not a divisive factor.[41] These developments demonstrate how sport and recreation organized by and for women at the grassroots level pose a significant challenge to the institution of compulsory heterosexuality.

Ice hockey player Justine Blainey, who in 1986
successfully challenged the section of the Ontario Human Rights
Code that excluded sex discrimination in sport.
Until this court decision, Justine had not been permitted to play
on a boys' hockey team.

CHAPTER SIX

EQUAL OPPORTUNITY
IN SPORT

THE FEMINIST MOVEMENT of the 1960s helped to bring to public attention the issue of female participation in contact sports, although equal opportunity in sport, and its significance in other areas of women's lives, was one of the last causes to mobilize feminists. However, two arguments were ultimately developed. Firstly, equality of opportunity in sport as in education or employment required that girls and women have access to all activities. In sport this would include contact sports such as soccer, football and hockey. Secondly, in order that girls and women might develop confidence in their bodies and take some responsibility for defending themselves against attack, specifically sexual assault, they needed instruction in self-defence techniques, such as those derived from combat sports or martial arts.

Many advocates failed — and still fail — to understand the relationship between these two rationales. Some feminists supported the training of girls and women in self-defence techniques, but gave the sport-related issues low priority. Similarly, some advocates of equal opportunity in sport did not support the rationale for women's self-defence. Ironically, the connection was often quite clear to the detractors, who correctly perceived the blurring of sex differences through equal opportunity in sport, particularly contact sports, as a slippery slope leading to the breakdown of traditional male/female power relations.

In the U.S.A., Title IX of the Education Amendments of 1972 prohibited discrimination on the basis of sex in any educational program receiving federal funds. The implementing regulation of 1975 required gender-integrated physical education classes in schools and universities, and provided for non-discrimination in the range of athletic activities, levels of competition, facilities, coaching and funding. However, there was an important loophole in the provision that sports designated as contact sports were permitted single-sex or male-only teams. In Canada, provincial human rights statutes offered similar protection. Ontario, the first province to enact a human rights code in 1962, was, in 1981, the first to introduce a clause exempting membership and participation in athletic organizations from its equality provisions. At the federal level, the Canadian Charter of Rights and Freedoms, which came into effect in 1985, prohibits discrimination based on sex.

The integration issue first arose in the late 1960s, when the debate over coeducational primary classes, even for academic subjects, was preoccupying many educators. Early in the century, girls were perceived to be the group in need of special treatment. By the 1960s, some educators, influenced by research on male homosexuality as well as psychology and pedagogy, advocated special provision for boys, especially in situations involving reading, writing or language, where their generally inferior performance compared to girls might cause them embarrassment or shame. Women teachers were blamed for handicapping boys "by expecting them to learn and behave like girls."[1]

Male teachers, as well as male peers, were central to the success of segregation: "There are no sweet little girls to crush [the boy's] efforts or to flaunt their successes before him. He is with men and he likes it."[2] Girls' strengths — neatness, attention to detail, orderly behaviour in class, helpfulness to other children — were devalued in order to present boys' undeniably masculine traits — disorderliness, loudness and aggression — in a more positive light. Needless to say, girls' weaknesses were seldom transformed in this way, nor was segregation recommended to protect girls from public failure.

In such an atmosphere, the concept of mixed sport and physical education was not likely to be well received: if girls' superior intellectual ability threatened the fragile male ego, how much more dangerous was the possibility of female equality, or even superiority, in the male domain of sport. In equal jeopardy was the role of sport in establishing masculine identity, which, it seemed, was as shaky as male ego. According to one male recreation commissioner, "This unisex thing is going too far ... boys don't even know they're boys any more."[3] Many advocates of sex-differentiated programs invoked parental rights and "the sanctity of the home," blaming feminists and lesbians for instigating the move towards integration and the attack on the masculine sex role.[4]

In the U.S.A., the Title IX regulation of 1975 designated baseball a contact sport, permitting the exclusion of females from school or university teams even though girls could play on mixed community teams.[5] Subsequent attempts were made by opponents of integration to have most team sports designated contact sports.[6]

Opposition to coeducational contact sports — and virtually all team sports were classified as "contact" — ostensibly rested on safety concerns, although attitudes and practices related to integration clearly reflected and reinforced patriarchal ideology. Despite physiological evidence to the contrary, it was consistently argued that females, being weaker than males, would sustain injuries in mixed sports. "There would be a far greater emotional impetus [sic] when a girl gets hurt, as against a boy."[7]

Sex differences in speed, strength and endurance after puberty obviously had to be considered. Yet many studies showed minimal physical differences between pre-pubertal boys and girls. Moreover, the injuries that were predicted were, for the most part, sex-specific, involving breasts or genitals, rather than sport-specific. Obviously, female sex characteristics overrode more important considerations related to the size, strength and ability of the girls and women seeking entry to mixed teams. It was rarely acknowledged that the girls and women who were physically capable of playing on mixed teams were not the "average" females on whom most of the statistical findings were based.

Yet the vulnerability of the male genitals had never hampered male sporting participation. Protective equipment was developed to deal with the problem, and its use was adopted routinely and without fanfare. Clearly, female breasts or genitals could be similarly protected if athletes experienced pain or discomfort.

AN OFFENCE AGAINST PUBLIC DECENCY

One of the few publicly stated "moral" arguments against integrated sport, as it was phrased in 1972, claimed that "intimate body contact between opposite sexes at the adolescent age might offend some participants and/or observers."[8] More than ten years later, an Ontario government report claimed that "contact with the genital areas" in a sport such as rugby constituted an offence against "public decency."[9] Physical educators held that "physical contact" and "sexuality problems" were disadvantages of mixed physical education, and the sex of the instructor was also considered problematic. Contact with other-sex students during wrestling, for example, "could result in embarrassment or worse, misinterpretation which could lead to legal suits."[10]

The taboo against body contact between the sexes for other than sexual reasons mystifed the female body, glorified female modesty and sexualized even the most casual physical contact. These practices, however, did not protect girls and women against unwanted male attention or sexual assault; instead, they made females more vulnerable, since body contact, in the absence of mystery and modesty, constituted "asking for it."

Unfortunately, the connection between mixed contact sports and male/female relations has rarely been investigated by feminists. However, a convincing 1977 argument held that integrated sports have the effect of desexualizing contact between men and women by demonstrating that sexual arousal and intercourse are not necessarily the outcome of all hetero-sexual encounters that involve physical contact.[11] Arguably, "integration" of the workplace, or the school or university, produces the same result, but the actual physical closeness of contact sports makes the argument more persuasive. Indeed, if contact sports were sexualized, mixed practice and play would become impossible.

Significantly, neither the intimate contact among males nor the all-male environment of "manly sports" was perceived as having homosexual overtones. In fact, the relationships between coaches and players were a source of inspiration to many opponents of integration. This exalted "male bonding" also had a misogynist dimension; some volunteer male coaches threatened to quit if "forced" to accept girls.[12]

Evidently the sexual identity of male coaches was as much in need of validation through "manly sports" as that of the boys whom they instructed. The presence of girls on the team, it seemed, was seen as an intrusion on a sacred initiation ceremony. Such a fear was evident when Sue Palmer first participated in intercollegiate basketball competition in 1974. Although her teammates accepted her, members of the opposing team, trailing in the second half, walked off the court, "murmuring obscene language and making childish signs with their hands" as soon as she stood up to play.[13]

Some educators advocated single-sex rather than integrated teams, in part to assuage male fear of being beaten by females. Others admonished boys to "be gentlemanly" or "help the girls out" in mixed games, thus devaluing girls' performance. If the girls were, in fact, superior, the boys had a convenient excuse in that they were not playing their best. Less chivalrous but equally effective was the practice of keeping girls out of the play, by refusing to pass the ball or puck in their direction.[14] Not all boys found the prospect of mixed play threatening: "If the guy gets beat, so what? If he can't admit a girl is better, he has a problem."[15]

A woman who invades male turf in sport (or business, or trade) is seen as rejecting the privileged, protected status of women who conform to the traditional feminine role. In male parlance, "She's got balls." This grudging compliment implies, however, that the woman thus endowed cannot expect male chivalry. At best, she is "one of the boys" and is expected to accept locker-room humour; at worst, she is fair game for verbal, physical or sexual abuse.

Although most supporters of girls' and women's sport opposed sex-specific programs that entrenched stereotyped activities, integration was not viewed as the solution to problems of sex inequality in sport. The strategy of single-sex sport offered women an alternative to the male model, which was criticized for its commercialization, elitism and violence. Some women in the 1980s opposed all aggression in sport, but just as many argued that the lessons learned on the playing field — team spirit, loyalty, cooperation, leadership ability, team strategy — prepared women for the male-dominated business world, where sport metaphors and sport mentality prevailed.[16]

It is tempting to suggest that women's sport, organized by women for women, would avoid all the pitfalls of men's sport, but there is no clear supporting evidence. It is popularly believed that, even if women's sport accepted commercial sponsorship and emphasized high performance, it would never develop the same violence as men's sport, because women are, by nature, less violent than men. (There is, of course, a distinction between the aggression intrinsic to contact sports, and rule-breaking violence.) Admittedly, women engage in fewer violent acts than men, but their opportunities for doing so, particularly in the context of sport, are considerably lower.[17]

Predictably, studies of women's teams coached by men in sports officiated and administered by men showed no clear trends towards a distinctly female model.[18] Moreover, many female coaches embrace male coaching methods wholeheartedly. As in any male-dominated field, the women promoted to leadership positions are often those whose approach is indistinguishable from men's. The few sports that are almost exclusively female at all levels — rhythmic gymnastics and synchronized swimming, for example — are not likely contexts for violence.

Incidents of female violence in contact sports were blamed on "imitative masculine machismo," allegedly a product of "women's liberation."[19] Such a polarized view of masculinity and femininity discredits the women's movement and assumes male supremacy. The notion that violence was a masculine "weakness" legitimizes the traditional view of women as men's moral superior, bearing the ultimate responsibility as peacemakers and moral guardians of society. It also reinforces the stereotype of women who enjoyed aggressive contact sports as both masculine and deviant.

There were women, as well as men, who argued that girls and women were not, or should not, be interested in contact or combat sports.[20] Under the provisions of Title IX, the question of mixed combat sports rarely arose, nor were institutions required to provide separate programs in boxing or wrestling. Bans against public female participation in contact sports exist in many states and provinces. The cultural taboo against women fighting affects all women, not only those interested in combat sports. It means that females have few opportunities to learn the fighting techniques needed to defend themselves against assault.

FIGHTING WOMEN

The Western combat sports of boxing and wrestling, based primarily on brute force, are effective against an opponent of approximately the same height, weight and strength. But some Eastern martial arts depend more on skill, mental energy and harmony, than on brute force, so that a person is better able to escape from or to overpower a stronger opponent. Therefore, while boxing and wrestling had obvious self-defence applications for some women, martial arts provided more useful preparation for defence against taller, heavier and stronger assailants.

The practice of Eastern martial arts in North America escalated dramatically in the late 1960s. Their popularity was fueled by a proliferation of movies and television shows which presented the martial artist as the new ideal of masculinity. The proportion of female karate students increased to 20 percent in the U.S.A. in 1973.[21] Since most training was conducted by men for men (and boys) in private clubs and on university campuses, cost, accessibility and physical requirements limited female participation. However, the most powerful barrier was the long-standing taboo against women engaging in physical fighting.

Physical grappling between men is seen as a celebration of masculinity and male bonding, but, between women, the act is considered unacceptable and unnatural, with sexual innuendos.[22] In this regard, there is a range of sexual interpretations. While the male scriptwriter for *Personal Best* used an arm-wrestling scene as a prelude to a lesbian relationship, a newspaper photographer used two Grey Cup beauty queens engaged in arm wrestling to promote the upcoming beauty contest, which was described as "a battle of pulchritude, not muscle."[23] Women's mud wrestling, of course, served as sexual entertainment for men.

These prohibitions against Western combat sport rarely applied to female participation in martial arts. Judo had some female involvement from the 1940s on, and was practised by women increasingly in the 1960s. Its introduction as a men's event in the 1964 Olympics probably increased its popularity at this time. A female equivalent to the male television hero, Honor Blackman, playing Cathy Gale in the British crime series *The Avengers*, used judo techniques in her acting and in writing one of the first women's self-defence guides. The same year, Ruth Horan, a New York YWCA judo instructor, published *Judo for Women*.

Rationales for female participation offered by Blackman, Horan and their contemporaries invariably mentioned the benefits to general health and beauty (including trimming the

Marilyn Walsh demonstrating a wendo technique.

waistline and hips) as well as judo's practical application against male attackers. Horan noted that "it would be wonderful if husband, brother, or boyfriend were always with us to protect and defend us," but "unfortunately," that was not always the case.[24]

A number of Korean and Japanese martial arts, including taekwon-do, hupkido, karate and aikido, became popular in North America by the 1970s. Women increasingly practised these for self-defence and because they enjoyed the physical and mental challenge of fighting. A hybrid form called wen-do was developed in Canada in 1972, mainly to provide women with an introductory 12-hour course in the basics of self-defence. Wen-do has been remarkably successful in reaching large numbers of women who might otherwise have had no preparation, although it was often presented in a way that implied a stereotype of women as unwilling or unable to spend time or energy on physical activity. Wen-do was frequently advertised as an easy skill that did not require physical fitness, style or strength — an important and valid claim, but not one to stimulate girls and women to develop the ease and confidence in their bodies and in their capacity to defend themselves that most boys and men acquire through sporting involvement.

By 1980, studies on body comportment and movement identified these sex differences and contributed insights on the relationships between female body experience and women's situation in sexist society. Feminist philosopher, Iris Young, proposed that a specific style of feminine comportment and movement is acquired at a young age as part of the general process of learning what it means to be a girl. Taught to view the body as a "fragile encumbrance," females develop a style characterized by a lack of "fluid and direct motion." Instead, "the motion is concentrated in one body part and ... tends not to reach, extend, lean, stretch and follow through," a pattern particularly evident in the feminine style of throwing, hitting a ball, or running.[25] Women engaged in self-defence martial arts have to "unlearn" this style, as the effectiveness of techniques applied to a taller, heavier opponent is maximized by putting one's whole body into each motion.

Women's disenchantment with male-dominated martial arts instruction was partly responsible for the development of wen-do, and led, in the early 1970s, to a "karate underground" of feminist-oriented schools for women in New York. The problems facing women in mixed classes ranged from condescension to retaliation. Male instructors refused to teach women certain skills that they considered "unfeminine," and male students used brute force to punch out female opponents who scored on them in sparring.[26] The "special treatment" did not serve women well, nor did facing a male training partner who refused, or claimed he was unable, to fight a woman.

The high proportion of Korean and Japanese men instructing in the martial arts was partly responsible for this approach. They tended to teach as they had been taught in the East, where women's instruction, if offered at all, was often an abridged

Wendo technique. Illustration by Iris Paabo.

version of men's. The responses of male students, however, reflected a purely North American brand of chauvinism. Rejecting a fellow student's sexual offer could result in "getting his fist in your face during the next day's class"; the same outcome could result from refusing a man with whom a woman was already involved.[27]

Wen-do and other women's self-defence instructors frequently warned students not to attempt these techniques on husbands or boyfriends. The common explanation was that, without the element of surprise, the technique would probably fail. What was rarely stated explicitly, however, was the possibility of retaliation if they were successful. In no other sport or physical activity was there such a raw confrontation between male domination and feminist resistance. The ability to defend herself does not make a woman a feminist, but fundamental issues of power crystallize around the image of the woman who fights back. While it may be commonly assumed that attackers are strangers on the street, women inevitably realize that any man — friend or relative, husband or lover, policeman or neighbour — is a potential assailant.[28] Women's consciousness of their power to fight back is as radicalizing an experience for contemporary women as it was for the British suffragists practising jiu jitsu.

I had the sense of well-being which comes from regular, strenuous exercise. I developed an agility in my movements and a resistance to fatigue and stress ... I began to feel like a person to be reckoned with, strong and competent. I began to feel powerful, emotionally and physically.

Linda Pearson,
"Learning to be a Survivor:
The Liberating Art of Tae Kwondo,"
Canadian Women's Studies
(Summer 1979): 49-50.

Many women experienced a new exhilaration and empowerment through integrating physical and mental energy in the practice of martial arts: "They want to be powerful and excellent without having to apologize for it." As one karate student stated,

"We *do* want to be Amazons — strong and beautiful women."[29] The reclaiming of the term Amazon was, of course, a new and positive trend.

Not all women shared this motivation, nor were all men prepared to grant women the right to be Amazons. According to a male judo instructor, "A woman's primary drive would naturally be self-defense. A few might take it up for physical conditioning, or as a sport."[30] One feminist karate student insisted that women "couldn't care less about proving themselves against men or about rising through the ranks to win belts to prove themselves."[31] Women, indeed, were learning to assert themselves by learning self-protection skills, but she failed to note that one way to achieve this goal was by progressing through the ranks and competing against men.

Claims that women were not interested in imitating or competing against men were particularly self-defeating when applied to martial arts. If defending herself effectively against male attack was, in fact, a woman's primary goal, none of the claims of female disinterest in aggressive, competitive contact sports was valid. To prepare herself for the most extreme acts of male aggression, it was essential that a woman learn to channel her own power, aggression and competitiveness effectively in her own defence.

From the mid-1960s on, as the rate of reported assaults and rapes escalated, some women and men were quick to associate the social and sexual freedom of the so-called "liberated" woman with indiscriminate risk-taking. "The tighter the bikini, the higher the miniskirt, the lower the cleavage, the more the danger ... Women may invite attack by wearing provocative clothing and by not exercising normal precautions in their actions."[32] A women's self-defence manual warned: "A woman who sexually excites a man and then stops him, claiming she's not 'that kind of girl,' deserves to be raped and sometimes is."[33] Evidently, "nice girls" did not get raped, and therefore "nice girls" need not learn self-defence. Fortunately, not everyone adopted this logic. In 1966, an Oregon police department offered a free self-defence training course for women, probably the first of its kind, and others soon followed its example.[34]

Resistance to women's self-defence continued into the 1980s, although there was ample evidence that women who were prepared to defend themselves were less likely to be assaulted or raped.[35] The exclusion of men from "Take Back the Night" marches symbolized a feminist alternative to isolation, passivity and dependence on men. The same solidarity was manifested through rape crisis centres, escort services on university campuses and self-defence courses; all were organized by women and for women.

While these developments were taking place in martial arts and self-defence, there were some parallels in Western combat sports. In Michigan, for example, wrestling and boxing were almost as popular among girls as judo and karate, and tackle football was only slightly less popular than synchronized swimming.[36] At higher competitive levels, however, there were formal barriers to women's participation: in New York state, for example, the Athletic Commission's ban on women's boxing was in effect until 1977. In Ontario, the Athletics Control Act prohibited female participation in amateur or professional boxing and amateur wrestling until 1985.

Where women's boxing was permitted, sex-specific regulations applied. In California, for example, heavier gloves were required, rounds were shortened, breast protection was mandatory, and contestants were required to affirm that they were not pregnant. Suzanne Hodgkiss, who set up the Ontario Women's Boxing Association in 1982, proposed that similar regulations be instituted in this province. The following year, the Ontario Amateur Boxing Review Committee, chaired by Bruce Kidd, recommended lifting the ban, as there was no evidence that female boxers faced an "unacceptably high" risk of injury.[37]

Qualified support came from one man: "Personally, I like my women pink and dainty, but if some women want to box, I don't see why men should have the authority to stand in their way."[38] Ontario Athletics Commissioner Clyde Gray stated his concerns regarding discrimination but added: "Who'd want to go to see a couple of females beat up on each other? Personally, I wouldn't want to have the responsibility of worrying about female boxers."[39]

Gray's comments indirectly raised the question of hetero-sexuality, as he seemed to imply that normal women would not enjoy female boxing, and normal men most certainly would not. Yet the question of spectators was, in part, a valid one, as professional boxing depended on a paying audience. But if boxing is a test of skill, and not a display of brutality, the gender of the contestants should not affect its entertainment value.

The most prominent public issue in female boxing was the belief that a blow to the breasts caused cancer. Neither the medical facts concerning traumatic breast cancer, nor the effectiveness of protective equipment, it seemed, could eradicate the myth. "Social and psychological reasons," rather than medical facts, caused women's exclusion from boxing.[40] Medical and psychological issues merged, however, on the question of sex-specific injury: "A unique problem of the female athlete relates to breasts."[41]

Increased female participation in all types of sports in the late 1970s sparked medical interest in the effectiveness of conventional bras during vigorous physical activity involving running or jumping, although early warnings of "sagging breasts" were, for the most part, dismissed by the 1980s.[42] Sportswear manufacturers produced a number of bras designed specifically for athletes. While books on women's running devoted considerable space to breasts and bras, advice to men rarely included ways of protecting their "unique" anatomy against discomfort or injury.

There are clear parallels between the traumatic breast cancer question in the 1970s and 1980s, and the uterine displacement question of the 1920s; in each case, medical opinion and practice depended on the context. Doctors were quick to warn against women's participation in sporting activities in which they might sustain injuries to the uterus or breasts, but were reluctant to allow that negligence on the part of employers or transportation companies could result in potentially dangerous trauma. In the sporting context, doctors treated the uterus and breasts as liabilities, prone to sex-specific diseases. When the issue of compensation arose, however, doctors seemed to suggested a view of women as dishonest and exploitative, intent on using the myths and mysteries of female anatomy for their own ends. In the first instance, doctors are protecting women from their own foolhardiness; in the second, they are protecting insurance companies from women's capriciousness.[43] It seems clear, however, that when human rights issues are at stake, and when adult women, not girls, are involved, individuals of both sexes should have the same freedom to engage in sports that carry an element of risk if they so choose.[44]

While such issues arose in relation to women's boxing, female participation in amateur wrestling was generally viewed as safer, and somewhat more desirable. A hybrid of wrestling and judo, sambo wrestling was included in the Pan-American games in 1983, marking women's first participation in combat sport in an international multi-sport competition. One feature of sambo wrestling might account in part for its acceptability for women: because the judo jacket is worn, rather than the more revealing leotard, the gender of participants is less obvious to spectators.

The issue of integrated wrestling was potentially controversial; educators often avoided the problem by eliminating it (and modern dance) from physical education curricula, rather than offering coeducational classes in activities traditionally associated exclusively with one sex. A more satisfactory solution was to provide integrated self-defence instruction.[45]

In Ontario high schools there were at least two instances where female students joined male wrestling teams in the absence of a female equivalent. One of these young women revealed her ambivalence: "On the mat I'm a competitor. Off the mat, I want them to treat me like a lady."[46] Perhaps, while male/female bodily contact was desexualized on the mat, she considered such contact, if it occurred off the mat, to have the usual sexual connotations, and she did not want her teammates to take advantage of this situation.

There is little doubt that amateur wrestling for both sexes has been tainted by professional wrestling as popularized by television. For women, there are additional problems; in the late 1970s, mud wrestling and nude wrestling, like striptease and table dancing, were forms of sexual entertainment for men. One aspiring promoter stated that he "wouldn't mind if it was done in good taste and on a respectable level with the wrestlers wearing a sleeveless leotard or perhaps a bikini." By 1982, riding on the fitness wave, he was promoting "a sportive, feminine, refined form of wrestling ... for sophisticated ladies, or liberated women, or sports/fun loving girls ... a physical fitness activity, primarily for fun and exercise."[47]

There were ethical considerations related to combat sports that pertained to both sexes; there was considerable opposition to any sport in which, allegedly, "the intent to injure" was central. The Ontario Amateur Boxing Review Committee concluded, however, that this was not true of amateur boxing; rather, the boxer's intent was "to dominate [the opponent] physically and make him feel his power." Regarding female participation, Kidd's position was that, if amateur boxing is good for males, it is good for females too.[48]

Moreover, a feminist argument questions whether adults have "the moral right to socialize children into activities which teach them to coolly, instrumentally, and efficiently inflict enough physical damage or effect enough physical force to dominate or intimidate another child in order to win a contest."[49] Given sportswomen's long tradition of opposition to boxing and to sport violence, women were seeking the freedom, not to participate in the sport system as it is, but "to reject the status quo in favor of an alternative system."[50]

This distinction between "equality" and "emancipation" parallels that between reform and revolution which feminists confront in the broader political context. As sportswomen have argued since the 1920s, it is not necessarily progressive to take all that is bad with all that is good from the male sporting model. Rather the goal is to have women's sport defined by and administered by women.

Developing a new ethos in women's sport is a goal that many women consider worthwhile. However, only a minority of women in sport approach the issue from a feminist perspective or take into account power relations between the sexes in the broader social and political context. Women are unlikely to transform the existing sport system unless they gain access to the decision-making process.

It is crucial that feminist arguments for woman-centred sport be distinguished from the reactionary position of sports administrators and others who refuse to allow integrated teams in contact sports. Feminists are certainly not arguing female frailty as grounds for separate teams, nor are they suggesting that women are morally superior and therefore have no interest in nasty, brutish, contact sports. However, blindly adopting the male model may not be the most effective way to achieve equality. Given equal opportunity in sport, women might transform the brutishness and revive the spirit of play.

♦

F*itness instructor Dawn Daniels at North Toronto Y.W.C.A., 1986.*

CHAPTER SEVEN

FIT AND FEMININE

BY THE 1970s, the fitness of North American men, women and children was becoming the focus of government programs and private enterprise. State interest stemmed in part from concerns for the health of citizens in an urbanized, industrialized society where sedentary lifestyles were the norm. In the private fitness industry, consumer interest sparked the proliferation of clubs, television shows, books, records and fashions — the marks of yet another successful capitalist enterprise.

When the benefits of aerobic exercise were first popularized by Kenneth Cooper in his 1968 publication, the low cardio-vascular fitness level of adult males was a major concern. [1] By the late 1970s, the fitness trend also encompassed the female population. Free community and school fitness programs were directed at girls and women of all socioeconomic backgrounds, while private fitness clubs focused on the needs, and the purchasing power, of middle-class women. Although most women probably experienced some health benefits from regular exercise, its liberating potential was marred by conservatism on the question of femininity and sexuality.

During the 1980s, women showed increasing interest in bodybuilding. This activity is quite distinct from weight training programs for a specific sport. Its function is primarily aesthetic: muscular development for its own sake. For women, the goal is to "sculpt" a thin, strong, muscular body that meets current standards of glamour. Although male bodybuilders are often criticized for their alleged narcissism, it is generally taken for granted that middle-class women devote time, money and effort to their appearance. Therefore, women's bodybuilding is often justified by the old "enhancement of femininity" rationale. Many private clubs offer dance exercise classes, fitness fashion boutiques and "esthetician" services, along with the weight training equipment, so their female clients may more fully pursue the new feminine ideal.

The President's Council on Physical Fitness and Sport (U.S.A.) announced in 1975 that the "modern girl's" participation in fitness activities — swimming, tennis, track, skiing — was producing "beautiful" results: "Her healthy glow, well-coordinated charm and educated grace come from Physical Fitness," it claimed.[2] The new ideal was "beautifully strong and fit," "taut, toned and coming on strong."[3]

Aerobic exercises provided, by "natural" means, the glow and grace formerly promised by cosmetic companies and fashion designers. Not surprisingly, the image of the physically active woman replaced the more sedentary and decorative 1960s ideal of heterosexual glamour. Women cycling, skiing, skating, swimming, snorkelling, horseback riding, playing tennis and volleyball appeared in advertisements for products as diverse as cigarettes, alcohol, convenience foods, diet products, life insurance, mattresses, cosmetics, clothing and "feminine hygiene" products.

Such ads firmly established the active woman's heterosexual identity by showing her more often in company of males than alone or with females. The men were usually assisting or admiring the perpetually smiling but frequently inept "sportswoman."[4] One perfume company even introduced "Le Sport" ("because life is a contact sport"). Ads showed women engaged in leisure activities with men: "Le Sport is more than a fragrance. It's a way of life. The look. The feeling. The vitality of the new sport life style. Day and night, you play with style." "Vitality," the ad announced, "is the new sex appeal."[5]

In feminine hygiene advertising, the new image of the active woman could have countered the myth that menstruation was an obstacle to strenuous physical activity; however, some ads served only to perpetuate the stereotype. Most showed a model, dressed appropriately but with the physique and style of an obvious non-athlete. Proclaiming "Stayfree Mini-Pads are so absorbent, I can get back to doing things I like sooner," one young woman was shown jumping the short distance from a rock to a river bank, apparently an activity she had to curtail during menstruation. Equally out of touch were the ads showing gymnasts in high-cut white leotards, supposedly demonstrating the invisibility of Stayfree Maxi-Pads. (This was, however, one of the few products promoted by a well-known female athlete, in this case American Olympic gymnast Kathy Rigby.)[6]

By 1984, aerobic dance or dance exercise had become one of the most popular physical activities of North American women. Also termed jazzercise, dancercise or slimnastics, it combined the aerobic elements of dancing, running and jumping with flexibility and strength exercises, all performed to contemporary music. While its popularity signified greater female participation in regular physical activity, its association with the cosmetic and fashion industries made it, in many instances, another arena for women to compete for male attention. Like makeup and clothing, dance exercise produced more prescriptions for heterosexual appeal. The new requirements included thinness, muscularity and shapeliness, enhanced by fashionable and expensive sportswear.

Competitiveness is not unusual, of course, in a sporting endeavour, so some degree of competitiveness in dance exercise was probably not surprising. Women of varying physiques and fitness levels, together in the gymnasium, change rooms and showers for the first time since their high school physical education days, undoubtedly made comparisons, both with one another and with the fitness ideal — the instructor. But dance exercise was supposedly non-competitive. It was developed for women, offered at convenient times and locales, in predominantly or exclusively female environments that promised to be supportive and non-threatening, especially to women new to physical activity. But many women felt pressured to lose weight, to work on specific body parts (thighs, hips, breasts) that fitness experts had diagnosed as a "problem," and to keep up with the instructor and the class, both in appearance and performance, regardless of individual goals, body type or fitness level.[7] By 1984, dance exercise had been fully transformed into a competitive female activity: "Aerobic Championships" were being staged across the country, conducted in shopping malls and promoted as "traffic builders."[8]

In many instances, the dance exercise instructor served as an example of both the fitness and the feminine ideal. She was probably white, slim and attractive, wearing the mandatory leotard, tights and legwarmers. Until organizations such as the American Aerobics Association and the Ontario Fitness Council began monitoring programs in 1982-83, instructors in private clubs were probably hired as much for appearance and style as for competence.[9] Some men were probably drawn to the classes, as spectators or participants, by the same considerations. Reducing the instructors to sex objects (especially the women on television "workout" shows) distorted and devalued the activity; many televised "classes" resembled soft porn rather than exercise.

Fashion was central to the coopting of dance exercise. Until the late 1970s, the leading North American manufacturer of leotards and tights, Danskin, was supplying these items to girls and women in ballet, modern dance and gymnastics, but its 1982 expansion into general exercise and fashion wear increased its sales dramatically.[10] The leotard's popularity among dance exercisers was probably due to its association with legitimate dance forms rather than the need for free, visible movement; less revealing clothing — shorts or track pants — would have satisfied these requirements without contributing to the self-consciousness of women who had not worn gym clothes since high school.

One of Danskin's early exercise products was the leotard with a high-cut leg, which its 1980 catalogue termed the diaper leg. Not coincidentally, advertisements for hair removal products at this time noted the "problem" of hair on the legs and "bikini line"; like bikinis, the high-cut leotard necessitated the removal of some pubic hair. The term "diaper leg" and the return to a child-like state of hairlessness signified the infantilization of the female body, a state hardly compatible with the empowerment that physical fitness might have brought to women.

With the entry of men into predominantly female dance exercise classes, the social dynamics changed. The escalating emphasis on youthfulness and thinness made some women feel uncomfortable. Others were ill at ease doing exercises which might have sexual connotations, especially when performed before a gallery of male spectators. Mixed dance exercise classes sometimes resembled a singles bar, while providing prospective partners with a very clear view of the other's physical condition. The fitness activities legitimized the social function, and, not surprisingly, some organizations responded by incorporating bars and restaurants into their multi-faceted operations.[11]

The association between dance exercise and heterosexual glamour was firmly established in 1982 when Jane Fonda headed a long line of celebrities who produced glossy, expensive fitness manuals. Sharing the Hollywood approach, some authors with more legitimate qualifications — prima ballerina Karen Kain and world-class marathoner Gayle Olinekova, for example — placed as much emphasis on becoming slim, trim and sexy as on staying fit.[12] If female athletes had the same commercial opportunities as males, either during or after their sporting careers, one would see books on exercise and training written by female athletes, rather than by actresses. Moreover, if a male counterpart to Jane Fonda or Raquel Welch — Robert Redford, for example — had written a book on running, it is unlikely that it would have had the credibility of the book by heart specialist and veteran marathoner George Sheehan, even though Redford is arguably a better example of "masculinity." This double standard reflects the assumption that men are serious about recreational sporting activities, while women are easily duped by passing fads and self-proclaimed experts, as long as the promise of heterosexual glamour is sufficiently seductive.

Serious female athletes who hope to endorse products, write sports columns or model sportswear are unlikely to succeed unless they conform to the feminine image. A 1983 *Runner* story on world champion marathoner Alison Roe, for example, was illustrated with bikini shots, presumably to boost Roe's modelling aspirations. Similarly, in *Sports Illustrated*'s annual swimsuit issues, glamour is obviously a more important factor than athletic prowess in the selection of models. Different rules apply to male athletes: sporting achievement apparently outweighs physical appearance when companies are looking for product endorsers or TV commentators.[13]

Despite the double standard, some female athletes succeeded on merit alone. Abby Hoffman, for example, wrote regular fitness columns in *Chatelaine* in 1980-82. These were factual, informative, and free of the usual emphasis on thinness and glamour that characterized the treatment of fitness in magazines such as *Glamour*, *Cosmopolitan* or *Ladies' Home Journal*.[14]

The active-woman image of the 1970s advertising had expanded by the 1980s to include the ubiquitous leotarded female figure, who by now symbolized female physical fitness and femininity in a variety of contexts. Ads for gyms and fitness clubs invariably featured leotarded women, often posing with male body builders flexing their muscles. This advertising made the heterosexual connotations quite clear through the juxtaposition of the figures and the seductive pose and expression of the woman.[15]

As with other representations of women as sex objects, such ads usually revealed far more of women's bodies than men's. One ad for karate classes, for example, showed a man wearing the traditional martial arts uniform instructing a woman clad only in a leotard. This unlikely situation conveyed either that women were not serious students, or that karate was primarily a fitness activity.[16]

Many women showed resistance to the media image of female physical fitness and the monopoly of the private fitness industry. Conscious of exploitative practices, informed women selected those facilities and services best suited to their individual ability. Many successful programs, organized by and for women, were sensitive to women's diverse fitness needs. To counter the emphasis on youthfulness in dance exercise classes, programs were developed for older women, while yoga or walking were often recommended as alternatives. Some instructors, rejecting the "Barbie doll" image, chose alternatives to the leotard and tights uniform. A British Columbia woman established exercise classes for women who, like herself, were overweight; her purpose was to provide exercise in a comfortable setting, with no expectations of weight loss. Early in 1984, two London, Ontario, women set out to establish a feminist health and fitness counseling centre that would provide a "non-sexist, educational, individually-oriented atmosphere" and be accessible to all women and girls.[17]

FEMININE MUSCLES ONLY

The 1980s active-woman image was lean and muscular, in contrast to her softer, more rounded 1970s counterpart. This change had implications for the clothing industry, as fitness clothing and the physique associated with fitness training became fashionable.

> [The models] were taut, toned with the kind of clearly defined musculature that speaks of a commitment to fitness, that says quite clearly, 'I am muscle'. The overall effect, not surprisingly, was erotic and very feminine.
>
> Paul Howard and John MacKay,
> "Singing the Body Eclectic,"
> *Toronto Life Fashion* (Summer 1982): 58.

Equating muscle with femininity and eroticism was not necessarily progressive; it could easily be distorted and coopted as yet another measure of heterosexual glamour among competing women. A female fitness instructor, Selby Pilot, asserted that bodybuilding, done "properly," enhanced femininity: "You can sculpt your body, build size, definition and structure." A male fitness instructor disagreed, claiming that women were "meant to have a layer of fat," and that female bodybuilders, lacking that "rounded" dimension, were "pseudowomen."[18] The low body fat of competitive female bodybuilders when compared to most other groups of female athletes and, more importantly, to the general female population, probably accounted for the image of bodybuilders as having relatively flat, muscular chests (hence, the label "pseudowomen"). The broad shoulders, narrow waist and hips of some bodybuilders were obviously a departure from the usual feminine figure, although body type was partly responsible.[19]

Bodybuilder Christina Dutkowski at Mac's Gym, Toronto.
Dutkowski holds the world bench press record for women.

Despite public preoccupation with sex appeal, female body-builders did not necessarily view the muscle issue in terms of pleasing men: "I don't do it for them in the first place" was one such response.[20] Yet bodybuilding was often promoted as a way of developing chest muscles, and, by inference, sexual allure. A Michigan bodybuilder and author of *Getting Built* stated: "If I didn't lift weights I wouldn't have a cleavage."[21]

There were, of course, inherent rewards in weight training, just as in any sporting endeavour: the sense of achievement, obvious gains in strength and an enhanced body image. One female bodybuilder proposed that these were feminist goals.

... this is a natural outgrowth of feminism, to be concerned, respectful and proud of our bodies, and to build a healthy relationship between our bodies, minds and sexuality ... Muscles are a metaphor for mental strength and achievement.

Trixie Rosen,
Strong and Sexy: The New Body Beautiful
(New York: Delilah, 1983), p. 9.

The goal of developing one's full physical potential — muscular strength, endurance, flexibility, even beauty — was obviously compatible with the general goal of self-actualization, and thus with feminist principles. In a Pittsburgh affirmative action program, for example, weight training was one component of a course which prepared unemployed women for high-paying positions as steelworkers.[22] While developing muscles in order to get a better job, or to play a better game, or to increase self-esteem, might reflect feminist consciousness, the same is hardly true of posing in a bikini before a panel of judges in a "beautiful muscle" contest.

By the 1980s, general fitness books for women were including advice on weight training programs, and the mandatory fitness sections in women's magazines were treating weight training as the latest step in toning "the body beautiful": "No, body building won't make you a female Conan the Barbarian — just shapelier, firmer, *sexier*!"[23]

From the time of the first National Women's Body Building Championships, held in California in 1979, a debate raged over "athletic" versus "aesthetic" muscle development, a new variation on the old masculine/feminine debate. Some commentaries labeled the early events beauty contests; some competitors, it was claimed, never lifted weights.[24] Most prize-winners, even five years later, had aesthetic/feminine muscle — smooth, sleek, well-toned and with sufficient body fat to ensure conventional feminine shapeliness. The offending "masculine" physique was characterized by the "low-fat, striated-muscle look" of muscles traditionally associated with men, visible and prominent even when not "pumped up."[25] Charles Gaines, a bodybuilder and author, offered a more detailed description: "veiny, chunky, stand-out," "rippled, delineated, vein-splayed," "ridged" and "ropy." The founder of the Women's Bodybuilding Association, George Snyder, called women with this kind of muscle "freaks."[26]

Masculine muscles, big shoulders and small hips made a minority of women in bodybuilding look "like small men," according to Doris Barrilleaux, founder of the American Federation of Women Bodybuilders. She claimed that judges who awarded prizes to these masculine bodybuilders were responsible for the escalating use of steroids.[27] Gaines maintained that masculine muscles were not winning prizes, product endorsements, positions in the Federation, or male approval. He claimed, however, that the unpopularity of this kind of bodybuilding was reducing competition once more to the level of beauty contests. Therefore, he favoured "the unhindered development and competition of female muscle" that the trend towards so-called masculine muscles represented.[28]

The debate had direct implications for actual competition. Despite some assertions that there was a spirit of support and cooperation amongst female bodybuilders, several articles reported incidents of hostility, especially in relation to women with masculine physiques. A fight was reported between two contestants in an Oshawa competition, "spurred by taunts of 'lesbian' and 'ugly'"; the judges had told contestants "they wanted muscularity with femininity," a requirement which the winner, a ballet dancer, obviously satisfied. In another contest, the judge dismissed one disappointed bodybuilder with the comment, "She's gone too far."[29]

None of the issues in this debate was new; as early as 1912, attempts were made to classify female body types and their relation to sporting participation. The stereotypes suggested by this classification were remarkably similar to those operating today. The "conventional" or "feminine" woman had "a narrow waist, broad and massive hips and large thighs," and the "athletic" or "masculine" type had more muscular, powerful limbs and trunk, with less accentuated "sex characteristics," and an enlarged chest expansion and waistline.[30] Apparently athletic women were masculine and asexual; non-athletic women were feminine and heterosexually appealing.

In summary, many of the objections to the masculine style of bodybuilding were traditional ones. Women were attempting to look or act like men, and therefore were unattractive, unnatural, freakish, or lesbian. Not only were these women entering a traditionally male activity; they were also challenging the sex-differentiated standards that were the conditions of their entry. Thus, it is not surprising that non-conformity to the feminine image was controversial. However, the aesthetic criteria of women's bodybuilding change with standards of heterosexual attractiveness, as well as affecting these standards. Fitness trends also play a part, of course. A degree of thinness and muscularity which, twenty years ago, was incompatible with femininity or heterosexual appeal is now an accepted standard among most middle-class women.

Women's increasing participation in fitness-related activities, from dance exercise to bodybuilding, is potentially liberating. To feel at ease with one's body and to be aware of its strengths and weaknesses is to know oneself better. Moreover, the sense of achievement derived from visible fitness gains encourages women to tackle other physical or mental challenges. For over a century, however, masculine/athletic versus feminine/aesthetic considerations, defined by males and serving male interests, have constrained female participation and coopted many fitness activities in the service of compulsory heterosexuality.

WOMEN HAVE THE LAST WORD

THROUGHOUT THE CENTURY of women's sporting participation in North America, there have been sustained attempts on the part of the dominant male group to control the female reproductive function and female sexuality. Sport threatened the male monopoly over female health, physicality and sexuality. The woman who was competent in sport challenged the female frailty myth and the illusion of male supremacy. She refused to be a victim of a "unique" biology that fitted her only for motherhood. And the woman who exercised physical and sexual independence posed a challenge to compulsory heterosexuality; she did not organize her life around male protection and male admiration.

Medical professionals played a major role in determining those sports and levels of participation that were safe for female anatomy and physiology. Not coincidentally, these activities were seen to enhance femininity, a socially constructed and historically specific concept encompassing personality, appearance and comportment. Acceptable activities promoted the physical and the psychological characteristics that males, as the dominant sex, pronounced appropriate and appealing for females: general and reproductive health, heterosexual attractiveness, passivity and conformity. On all of these issues, physical educators, sports administrators, journalists and the general public treated medical opinion as the voice of reason and authority.

The fertility of white, middle-class women was the primary focus of medical attention, although medical control of the female reproductive function extended to all women regardless of class and race. That girls and women, unknowingly or deliberately, might jeopardize their childbearing capacity through sporting participation continues to preoccupy sports gynecologists. Medical attitudes and practices reflect and reinforce the axiom that motherhood is the destiny of *all* women, and its corollary, that all women must be fertile all the time. Other possibilities were either dismissed or ignored; women might welcome a temporary cessation of menstruation, or might give priority to an athletic career over motherhood, or might choose lesbian rather than heterosexual expression of their sexuality. And indeed many sportswomen resisted male control of their sexuality and reproductive function in precisely these ways.

Although doctors were quick to blame middle-class women's sporting activities for infertility and "lost femininity," they were reluctant to acknowledge the threat posed by hazardous working conditions to the reproductive health — or even the general health — of working-class women, least of all to their femininity. By enforcing this class double standard, some medical and legal authorities diverted public attention away from the exploitation of female workers and the negligence of employers.

Compulsory heterosexuality was fundamental to the processes by which sport became yet another arena for male control and female resistance on questions of reproduction and sexuality. As well as legitimizing medical attitudes and practices related to fertility and motherhood, the concept of heterosexuality invoked criticism of women who did not meet prescribed standards of femininity. Sex differentiation was the guiding principle; whatever was appropriate in appearance, behaviour or deportment for men was automatically inappropriate for women. Such prescriptions, promoted by sport administrators and journalists, discouraged female participation in "masculine" sports and discredited the camaraderie among sportswomen by allegations of lesbianism. Furthermore, entrepreneurs in the fitness industry coopted activities such as dance exercise and bodybuilding by promising glamour as well as health and fitness.

Efforts to preserve sport as a bastion of male supremacy were, of course, proportionate to the threat posed by a movement that offered women the chance to develop to their full physical potential. Even the most ardent critic of women's sport would probably acknowledge that socially imposed restrictions on girls' and women's physical activities were a major factor in keeping their performance levels far below males, (although the most reactionary would also argue that these were "natural" or divinely ordained arrangements that should not be altered).

It has served male interests to stress biological differences, and to ignore the more numerous and obvious biological similarities between the sexes. The effective channeling of males into masculine sports and females into feminine sports maximized sex differences and entrenched the masculine/feminine dichotomy. "Manly" sports made a boy into a man while the activities offered to girls merely served health and beauty functions. If the development of personal potential were the goal, it would seem reasonable to encourage girls and women to play sports that promote speed, strength and endurance, and to provide boys and men with activities that develop grace, flexibility and balance.

In the early 1900s, women's athletic performances did not constitute a serious threat to male supremacy, but by the 1980s

Illustration from Benjamin Austin, ed.,
Woman: Her Character, Culture and Calling
(Brantford: Book and Bible House, 1898).

researchers predicted that female athletes would eventually equal male records in many sports. Not surprisingly, these trends caused considerable concern. Men might no longer enjoy the power and privilege accorded the dominant sex; women might no longer find comfort in the patriarchal myth that femininity had its own rewards — male approval and protection.

Female participation in those activities considered to be aesthetically pleasing — figure skating, rhythmic gymnastics and synchronized swimming, for example — was rarely if ever associated with loss of femininity, while contact, combat and team sports were blamed for promoting undesirable and unfeminine traits in female participants. A major difference between masculine and feminine sports lay in the participant's presentation of herself: whether she performed as an individual or as a member of a team, whether attention was focused on her appearance or solely on her performance, and whether the activity involved a public display of aggression.

The designation of certain sports as masculine had clear ideological implications. In patriarchal societies, the role of aggressor and protector is assigned to the male, and female participation in sports that involve aggression is seen as an unnatural role reversal. The ideal family provides male protection for its female members and these arrangements are reinforced by the conditions of men's and women's lives. In industrial capitalist society, women work in isolation in the private, domestic sphere, while men's public, cooperative endeavours facilitate alliances within social classes, as well as alliances of the dominant sex that often cross class lines. When women *do* work outside the home, they add to this workload the domestic work within the home that has long been their primary responsibility.

Contemporary women in the western world continue to experience isolation and, although the feminist movement has partially succeeded in promoting solidarity among women, differences in class, race, religion and sexual preference continue to cause rifts. Constrained by their double work day, women often lack the time for sustained political action. Moreover, childhood socialization does little to prepare women for the team effort that is required of feminist activists. Experience in team sports equips boys for the male-dominated world of business and politics as presently constituted. Given the opportunity, women might put team sport experience to use in the same way, or might work towards transforming politics, business and sport.

The classification of individual, aesthetically pleasing sports as feminine reflects the primacy given to heterosexual appeal in any context in which female performance is evaluated. When women conform to current standards of attractiveness, masculinity, both individual and collective, is validated, as is the competition between individual women for male attention and protection. In this system, there is no place for teamwork and solidarity among women. Moreover, femininity in sport militates against authentic expressions of physical and mental strength; it requires artifice, a deliberate effort to convey ease, grace and charm. Masculinity in sport is less dependent on artifice, makeup or play-acting; it does not carry the same expectation that concentration or strain be concealed behind a bland, smiling mask.

Female participation in team sports poses a double threat: women may apply the principles of cooperation and solidarity learned on the playing field to other social contexts, and they may subsequently challenge the longstanding male tendency to evaluate women's appearance before their performance. That lesbians may participate in team sports (as, of course, they do) poses yet another threat to male supremacy, by rendering male attention and approval redundant.

By rejecting "feminine" sports and the "feminine" image, many female athletes are publicly giving performance and achievement precedence over charm and popularity. However, as media coverage and the corporate sponsorship of sports play an increasingly powerful part in determining athletes' careers, the cost to these women is likely to be high. It has been a common tactic to discredit female athletes, especially those who played traditionally male sports, by accusing them of imitating men, or of being lesbians. In either case, these women, allegedly unattractive to men, will not receive the benefits that are granted to their more conforming, more "feminine" counterparts.

This is not to suggest that women collaborate in their own oppression. Rather, patterns of sex differentiation within sport have a deceptive aura of common sense and naturalness. They reflect and reinforce "what is," in terms of relations between the sexes: females are the smaller, slower, weaker sex, needing the protection of the bigger, stronger, faster men. Therefore, the argument goes, women should participate in the activities to which they are naturally suited — individual, aesthetically pleasing activities that show their beauty and grace to good effect while making relatively small demands on strength and endurance. The alternative strategy, encouraging participation in the areas in which each sex is weaker, with the goal of equalizing performance and promoting full human potential, provides a tantalizing glimpse of "what might be."

Although significant changes have taken place over the past hundred years in women's sport, underlying assumptions regarding women's physical inferiority continue to operate. Ideological leadership on these issues continues to rest with the predominantly male medical professionals, sports administrators and sports journalists. That the leadership is not exclusively male does not, of course, pass unnoticed. Some women's apparent complicity in supporting discriminatory practices is used to prove two myths: that women are "their own worst enemies," or that females are incapable of competing on equal terms with males. Rather, such acquiescence to male control simply indicates the relative powerlessness of women in the male-dominated sport system.

Sport both dramatizes and reinforces power relations between the sexes. Therefore, woman's place in sport does not differ significantly from her place in the family, the school, the workplace or the political system, for all of these institutions play a part in shaping sport. The potential for change, however, is present in all of these contexts, and indeed within sport itself, and many historical and contemporary trends initiated by women have effectively countered male control.

Some women are working towards changing discriminatory rules and practices in schools, universities and sport organizations. Others are establishing women-only sporting activities as alternatives to those in which the leadership — coaching, officiating and administration — is controlled by men and ordered by traditional male values. Women and men are questioning the professional sport system that too often glorifies violence, cheating, commercialism and a win-at-all-costs mentality. And feminists are challenging the sexist and heterosexist assumptions that underlie reactionary criticisms of strong, independent sportswomen. The process of transforming sport has begun.

NOTES

Abbreviations:
JAMA: Journal of the American Medical Association
JOHPER: Journal of Health, Physical Education and Recreation
JOPERD: Journal of Physical Education, Recreation and Dance

INTRODUCTION

1 Catharine MacKinnon, "Feminism, Marxism, Method, and the State: An Agenda for Theory," *Signs* 7,3 (1982), pp.532-3.
Men here are defined as members of a "gender group characterized by maleness as socially constructed."

2 Recent developments in neo-Marxist theory provide an appropriate theoretical framework for analyzing these processes: for example, Gramsci's concept of hegemony, elaborated upon by neo-Marxist theorists in the sociology of education and the sociology of sport.
See Antonio Gramsci, *Selections from the Prison Notebooks*, edited and translated by Quintin Hoare and Geoffrey Nowell Smith (New York: International Publishers, 1971), pp.325-9, 421-5; Richard Gruneau, *Class, Sports and Social Development* (Amherst, Massachusetts: University of Massachusetts Press, 1983); Paul Willis, "Women in Sport in Ideology," in Jennifer Hargreaves, ed., *Sport, Culture and Ideology* (London: Routledge Kegan Paul, 1982), pp.117-35.

3 Adrienne Rich, "Compulsory Heterosexuality and Lesbian Existence," *Signs* 5,4 (1980), pp.631-60.

CHAPTER ONE

1 For a comprehensive history of gynecology in the U.S.A., see Barbara Ehrenreich and Deidre English, *For Her Own Good: 150 Years of the Experts' Advice to Women* (Garden City, New York: Anchor Books, 1979). For historical developments in Canada, see Wendy Mitchinson, "Historical Attitudes Towards Women and Childbirth," *Atlantis* 4,2 Part 2 (Spring 1979), pp.13-34, and "Gynecological Operations upon Insane Women, London, Ontario, 1895-1901," *Journal of Social History* 15,3 (Spring 1982), pp.467-84.

2 Frances Kidd, "Is Basketball a Girls' Game?" *Hygeia* 13 (September 1935), p.834. *Hygeia* was a publication of the American Medical Association intended for general readers.

3 George Engelmann, "The American Girl of Today," *American Journal of Obstetrics* 42 (December 1900), p.759. Engelmann was president of the American Gynecological Society at the time.

4 Edward Clarke, *Sex in Education, or A Fair Chance for Girls* (Boston: J.R. Osgood, 1873), p.82; John Cowan, *The Science of a New Life* (New York: Ogilvie, 1919), p.361.

5 Howard Kelly, *Medical Gynecology*, 2nd ed. (New York: D. Appleton, 1913), pp.311-12, 315. See also Patricia Vertinsky, "The Effect of Changing Attitudes Toward Sexual Morality upon the Promotion of Physical Education for Women in 19th Century America," *Canadian Journal of History of Sport and Physical Education* 7,2 (1976), pp.26-38.

6 See, for example, the views of American gynecologist John Todd quoted by G. Barker-Benfield in *The Horrors of the Half-Known Life* (New York: Harper and Row, 1976), p.209.

7 Flora Denison, "Reform in Woman's Dress," *Woman's Century* (Special Number, 1918), p.45.

8 Max Huhner, *A Practical Treatise on the Diseases of the Sexual Function*, 2nd ed. (Philadelphia: F.A. Davis, 1923), pp.42-3, 53.

9 See, for example, Arabella Kenealy, "Woman as an Athlete," *Living Age* 3 (May 1899), pp.368-9; "Woman as an Athlete: A Rejoinder," *Living Age* 4 (July 1899), p.204. For a rebuttal to Kenealy, see "Woman as an Athlete: A Reply to Dr. Arabella Kenealy," *Living Age* 3 (June 1899), pp.799-806.

10 Angenette Parry, "The Relation of Athletics to the Reproductive Life of Woman," *American Journal of Obstetrics* 66 (September 1912), pp.348-9.

11 John Kellogg, *Plain Facts for Young and Old* (1888; New York: Arno Press, 1974), p.597.

12 Kenealy, "Woman as an Athlete," pp.366-7.

13 Wellesley study cited by R. Tait McKenzie, *Exercise in Education and Medicine*, 3rd ed. (Philadelphia: W.B. Saunders, 1923), p.278. Vassar study cited by Willystine Goodsell, *Pioneers of Women's Education in the United States* (New York: McGraw-Hill, 1930), p.126.

McKenzie, physical director at McGill University in Montreal, observed a relationship between athletic achievement and academic standing among female students in the gymnastic program. See R. Tait McKenzie, "Report on Physical Education at McGill," 1892, cited in Margaret Gillett, *We Walked Vary Warily* (Montreal: Eden Press, 1981), p.103.

14 Lucy Hall, "The Tricycle for Women," *The Chautauquan* 12 (October 1890), pp.90-1.

15 Grace Ritchie, "Discussion," *National Council of Women of Canada Yearbook, 1895* (Montreal: John Lovell, 1896), pp.116-17.

16 *The Family Physician, or Every Man His Own Doctor*, compiled by Leading Canadian Medical Men [sic] (Toronto: Hunter Rose, n.d.), p.172. It is estimated that this book was published between 1890 and 1905. See also Arthur Edis, *The Diseases of Women* (Philadelphia: Henry Lea's Sons, 1882); Charles Penrose, *Diseases of Women and Gyneocology* (New York: W.B. Saunders, 1904).

17 See, for example, Mary Jacobi, *The Question of Rest for Women during Menstruation* (New York: Putnam's, 1877); Clelia Mosher, *Health and the Woman Movement*, cited in Goodsell, pp.298-9; Mosher, "A Physiologic Treatment of Congestive Dysmenorrhea and Kindred Disorders Associated with the Menstrual Function," *JAMA* 62 (April 1914), pp.1297-1301; Alice Clow, "Menstruation during School Life," *British Medical Journal* 2 (October 1920), pp.511-13.

18 Engelmann, "The American Girl," pp.782-3.

19 E.H. Arnold, cited by Goodsell, p.299. In a two-year experiment conducted at the New Haven Normal School, Dr. Arnold reduced the time lost to menstrual incapacity in all sports except swimming. His major interest, however, was the reduction of absenteeism among working women. Estimating that one-sixth of their time was lost to menstrual incapacity, he argued that women were only justified in seeking equal pay if they actually worked the same hours as men.

20 John Hastings, "Are We Giving the Child a Square Deal?" *Woman's Century* (Special Number, 1918), p.152.

21 Jacobi, *The Question of Rest*, pp.227-32.

22 Mosher, "A Physiologic Treatment," pp.1297-1301.

23 See, for example, Clow, "Menstruation," pp.511-13.

24 Norman Miller, "Additional Light on the Dysmenorrhea Problem," *JAMA* 95 (December 1930), pp.1796-1801. See also Ruth Ewing, "A Study of Dysmenorrhea at the Home Office of the Metropolitan Life Insurance Company," *Journal of Industrial Hygiene* 13 (September 1931), pp.244-51; the stated purpose of Ewing's study of 500 office workers was to reduce lost work hours.

25 Parry, "The Relation of Athletics," p.347.

26 See, for example, Cowan, *The Science of a New Life*, pp.318-19; F. Davenport, *Diseases of Women: A Manual of Gynecology* (Philadelphia: Lea Brothers, 1898), p.190; Robert Dickinson, "The Corset: Questions of Pressure and Displacement," *New York Medical Journal* (November 1887), pp.507-16.

27 Gynecologists' responses cited by Parry, "The Relation of Athletics," pp.352-3.

28 Lists from *Healthful Schools*, co-authored by Jesse Williams, reprinted in Jesse Williams, *Personal Hygiene Applied*, 6th ed. (Philadelphia: W.B. Saunders, 1940), p.182.

29 Ethel Cartwright, "Physical Education and the Strathcona Trust," *The School* 4 (January 1916), pp.306-10.

30 Senda Berenson, cited by Elisabeth Halsey, *Women in Physical Education* (New York: Putnam's, 1961), pp.158, 160.

31 Nora Cleary, interviewed by Marjory Murdock in 1939 and cited by Helen Gurney, *Girls' Sport: A Century of Progress* (Don Mills, Ontario: Ontario Federation of School Athletic Associations, 1979), p.21.

32 Chicago gynecologist Harry Mock investigated these compensation cases in 1922; see "So-Called Traumatic Displacements of the Uterus," *JAMA* 79 (September 1922), pp.797-804.

33 On the displacement question, a 1922 study reported that "uncomplicated retroposition" of the uterus occurred in 22 percent of unmarried women; these cases were congenital, and unrelated to pathological or physiological factors. See Leda Stacy, "Anteposition and Retroposition of the Uterus: Incidence and Symptoms," *Mayo Clinic Collected Papers* 24 (1922), pp.393-7.

34 William Anderson, *Anderson's Physical Education* (Toronto: Harold Wilson, n.d.), p.20. It is estimated that this book was published around the turn of the century.

35 McKenzie, *Exercise in Education*, pp.76, 286-7.

36 Frederick Rand Rogers, "Olympics for Girls," in Women's Division, National Amateur Athletic Federation, ed., *Women and Athletics* (New York: Barnes, 1930), p.77 (excerpt from Rogers' 1929 article in *School and Society*).

37 A survey of 1,200 Smith College graduates found that the level of participation in college athletics bore no significant relationship to difficult pregnancies or labours. See Linda Gage Roth, "Are Sports Harmful to Women?" *The Forum* 81 (May 1929), pp.313-18.

38 Tait McKenzie was a pioneer of exercise therapy.

39 Interview (February 1983) and personal files, Gladys Gigg Ross, a participant in 1930 British Empire Games track and field events.
  Dr. Arthur Lamb, who succeeded Tait McKenzie as physical director at McGill, was one of several delegates to the 1928 International Amateur Athletic Federation who opposed the continuation of certain Olympic track and field events for women. Ironically, Lamb was also manager of the highly successful Canadian women's track team.

40 See, for example, R. Tait McKenzie, "The Functions and Limits of Sport in Education," *Canadian Medical Association Journal* 16 (June 1926), p.631; Leopold Shumaker and William Middleton, "The Cardiac Effects of Immoderate College Athletics," *JAMA* 62 (April 1914), pp.1136-44. For a summary of findings, see Percy Dawson, *The Physiology of Physical Education* (Baltimore: Wilkins and Wilkins, 1935), pp.898-9.

41 See James Whorton, "'Athlete's Heart': The Debate over Athleticism, 1870-1920," *Journal of Sport History* 9,1 (1982), pp.30-52. One of the earliest North American studies of women's cardiovascular capacity, conducted in 1922, was reported by Marie Damez, Percy Dawson et al., "Cardiovascular Reactions in Athletic and Nonathletic Girls," *JAMA* 86 (March 1926), pp.1420-2.

42 *Index Medicus* provided translated titles which gave an indication of international trends. In 1926, for example, it listed 14 articles on exercise therapy, compared to only one in 1919. German articles included two from the first volume of *Sportmedizin* (1929), one on the value of sport during menstruation and the other on the female constitution and athletics. A 1928 German article discussed excluding women from sport, followed in 1929 by one on excessive gymnastics as a cause of female sterility. A summary of the German studies of the 1920s is provided by Dawson, pp.903-6.

43 Emilie Duentzer and Martha Hellendall, "The Influence of Physical Education Activities Upon Constitution, Child-Bearing and Menstruation of Women," translated by Carl Schrader, *Journal of Health and Physical Education* 1 (November 1930), p.47. See Ethel Cartwright, "Athletics and Physical Education for Girls," *Ontario Education Association Yearbook* (1923), pp.274-81.

CHAPTER TWO

1 See, for example Wayne Roberts, "'Rocking the Cradle for the World': The New Woman and Maternal Feminism, Toronto, 1877-1914," in Linda Kealey, ed., *A Not Unreasonable Claim* (Toronto: Women's Press, 1979), pp.15-46.

2 Arthur Lamb quoted by Elmer Ferguson in "I Don't Like Amazon Athletes," *MacLean's Magazine* 51 (August 1, 1938), p.32.

3 Donald Laird, "Why Aren't More Women Athletes?" *Scientific American* 154 (March 1936), p.142.

4 Agnes Wayman, *Education Through Physical Education* (Philadelphia: Lee and Febiger, 1934), pp.128-9.

5 Wayman, p.127.

6 C.H. McCloy, "A Study of Landing Shock in Jumping for Women," *Internationale Zeitschrift* 5 (1931), pp.100-11. The article also appeared in McCloy's own text *Philosophical Bases For Physical Education* (New York: P.S. Crofts, 1940). His criticism of doctors' tendency to blame jumping for displacement followed the same lines as Mock's 1922 argument. Mock, however, was trying to exonerate insurance companies, not women's sport — a crucial factor in the different receptions that each received from his colleagues.

7 McCloy, p.111.

8 Percy Dawson, *The Physiology of Physical Education* (Baltimore: Wilkins and Wilkins, 1935), p.901.

9 See, for example, Robert Dickinson, "Tampons as Menstrual Guards," *JAMA* 128 (June 16, 1945), p.492.

10 W.B. Hendry quoted by Frederick Griffin in "Sport Enhances Womanhood," *Toronto Star Weekly* (October 10, 1931), p.16.

11 Jane Madders, "Training for Childbirth — The Gymnast's Responsibility," *Journal of Physical Education* 42 (March 1950), p.14.

12 See, for example, Reginald Fitz, "The Modern Young Person," *Hygeia* 6 (June 1928), pp.307, 309.

13 Frank Richardson and Harriette Haynes, "Posture Correction in Late Adolescence: A Plan for Teaching Posture in a Girls' College," *Archives of Pediatrics* 51 (November 1934), pp.726-7.

14 J. Anna Norris, "Basket Ball — Girls' Rules," in *Women and Athletics*, pp.32-6.

15 Interview with Gladys Ross.

16 May Fogg, "A Girls' Program Organized for Character Education," in Jay Nash, ed., *Interpretations of Physical Education* Vol.3 (New York: Barnes, 1938), p.249.

17 H.E. Billig, "Dysmenorrhea: The Result of a Postural Defect," *Archives of Surgery* 46 (May 1943), pp.611-13; A.C. Dick, H.E. Billig and H.N. Macy, "Menstrual Exercises — Absenteeism Decrease and Work Efficiency Increase," *Industrial Medicine* 12 (1943), pp.588-9; John Haman, "Exercises in Dysmenorrhea," *American Journal of Obstetrics and Gynecology* 49 (1945), pp.755-61.

18 Haman, p.760, citing H. Ehrenfest's statement from "Menstruation and Its Disorders: A Critical Review of the Literature From 1933 to 1936 Inclusive," *American Journal of Obstetrics and Gynecology* 34 (1937), pp.699-729.

19 See, for example, Ruth Harris and C. Etta Walters, "Effect of Prescribed Abdominal Exercises on Dysmenorrhea in College Women," *Research Quarterly* 26 (May 1955), pp.140-6; Leir Golub et al., "Therapeutic Exercises for Teen-Age Dysmenorrhea," *American Journal of Obstetrics and Gynecology* 76 (1958), pp.670-4; Leir Golub, "A New Exercise for Dysmenorrhea," *American Journal of Obstetrics and Gynecology* 78 (1959), pp.152-6.

For a review of this research, see Violet Cyriax, "The Physiological Effect of Physical Exercise," *Journal of Physical Education* 41 (November 1949), pp.145-51.

20 *NORVOC* (Northern Vocational School Yearbook) for 1958, p.40, and *Toronto Star* clipping dated February 11, 1958, in Northern Vocational School scrapbook.

21 Ove Boje, "Doping: A Study of the Means Employed to Raise the Level of Performance in Sport," *Bulletin of the Health Organization of the United Nations* 8 (1939), pp.465-6.

22 For a review of the literature, see "Menstruation and Sport," *British Medical Journal* (December 21, 1963), p.1548; the review noted that there were often undesirable side effects of hormone use, but maintained that the advantages in cases of dysmenorrhea probably outweighed the risks.

23 A 1937 and a 1963 study cited in "Menstruation and Sport," p.1548.

24 E.J. Klaus, "The Athletic Status of Women," in E. Jokl and E. Simon, eds., *International Research in Sport and Physical Recreation* (Springfield, Illinois: Charles Thomas, 1964), pp.590-1. Klaus's conservative advice was based on research dating back to 1938.

25 See, for example, P.-O. Astrand et al., "Girl Swimmers," *Acta Paediatrica Scandinavica* Supplement 147 (1963), pp.10-12, 33-8; nearly one half of these women reported no effect of menstruation on performance.

26 Study reported by Dawson, *The Physiology of Physical Education*, p.905. Advertisements for Kotex booklet in *The School* (a Canadian teachers' journal) 1946-47, passim.

   In a 1959 survey of seventeen physicians and gynecologists, three recommended no swimming for any women during the early stages of the period, and eight restricted it for women suffering from menstrual problems. See Marjorie Phillips et al., "Sports Activity for Girls," *JOHPER* 30 (December 1959), pp.23-5, 54.

27 For a summary of survey findings, see Dickinson, "Tampons as Menstrual Guards," p.494.

28 Dickinson, p.490.

29 Irja Widenius, "A Study of Commercially Manufactured Catamenial Tampons," *American Journal of Obstetrics and Gynecology* 48 (1944), pp.510-22; see also Dickinson, p.494.

30 See, for example, Tampax advertisement in *Echoes* (Christmas 1943), p.25, and in most issues, 1941-45.

31 "Sports Opportunities for Girls and Women," (statement authorized by the American Medical Association's Committee on the Medical Aspects of Sports, May 1964), *JOHPER* 35 (November/December

1964), p.46; Jewell Nolen, "Problems of Menstruation," *JOHPER* 36 (October 1965), p.65. Nolen reported menstrual problems in 94 percent of female students in a Tennessee university survey. Stressing that menstruation was a "normal function," she suggested that either the problems were imaginary, or they were the result of faulty posture, poor hygiene and inadequate exercise. Compare Norris's advice to physical educators of the 1930s (note 14 above) to check for menstrual problems before permitting full sporting participation.

32 Theresa Anderson, "Swimming and Exercise During Menstruation," *JOHPER* 36 (October 1965), pp.66-8. Contrary to Anderson's review of the research, however, Astrand's study was one of the first to report an association between *intensive* training and irregular cycles in a minority of the swimmers surveyed. However, most retired swimmers had children and there was no evidence of an association between sterility and competitive swimming.

33 Report of the National Conference on Sportsmedicine, *South African Medical Journal* 53 (May 6, 1978), p.726.
   On the question of performance and menstruation, one of the first longitudinal studies of female Olympic athletes, conducted by Bulgarian physician Ekaterina Zaharieva, found that, depending on the event, 50 to 74 percent of those surveyed maintained their form during menstruation, 1 to 15 percent did worse than expected and 5 to 20 percent improved their performance. See Ekaterina Zaharieva, "Survey of Sportswomen at the Tokyo Olympics," *Journal of Sports Medicine* 5 (1965), pp.215-19.

34 This study, also by E.J. Klaus, is cited by R.M. Malina, "Menarche in Athletes: A Synthesis and Hypothesis," *Annals of Human Biology* 10 (1983), p.8.

35 See, for example, R.E. Frisch and R. Revelle, "Variations in Body Weights and the Age of the Adolescent Growth Spurt," *Human Biology* 41 (1969), pp.185-212; "Height and Weight at Menarche and a Hypothesis of Critical Body Weights and Adolescent Events," *Science* 169 (1970), pp.397-8; R.E. Frisch et al., "Delayed Menarche and Amenorrhea in Ballet Dancers," *New England Journal of Medicine* 303 (1980) pp.17-19. For a comprehensive analysis of twenty articles by Frisch and others on this issue, see Eugenie Scott and Francis Johnston, "Critical Fat, Menarche and the Maintenance of Menstrual Cycles: A Critical Review," *Journal of Adolescent Health Care* 2,4 (1982), pp.249-60.

36 See, for example, M. Grumbach, "Onset of Puberty," in S.R. Berenberg, ed., *Puberty* (Leiden: Stenfert Kroese, 1975), cited by Scott and Johnston, p.255; Michelle Warren, "The Effects of Exercise

on Pubertal Progression and Reproductive Function in Girls," *Journal of Clinical Endocrinology and Metabolism* 51,5 (1980), pp.1150-56.

37 Zaharieva, "Survey of Sportswomen," pp.215-19; Zaharieva, "Olympic Participation by Women: Effects on Pregnancy and Childbirth," *JAMA* 221 (August 28, 1972), pp.992-5;   James Webb et al., "Gynecological Survey of American Female Athletes Competing at the Montreal Olympic Games," *Journal of Sports Medicine* 19 (1979), pp.405-12.

On the question of fertility, 94 percent of Zaharieva's subjects gave birth after Olympic participation, and the majority reported no problems during pregnancy. After childbirth, more than 75 percent improved their pre-pregnancy performance. See also B.O. Eriksson et al., "Long-term Effect of Previous Swimming in Girls: A Ten-year Follow-up on the 'Girl Swimmers'," *Acta Paediatrica Scandinavica* 67 (1978), pp.285-92.

38 C.B. Feicht et al., "Secondary Amenorrhea in Athletes," *The Lancet* 2 (November 25, 1978), pp.1145-6.

39 American College of Sports Medicine Opinion Statement on "The Participation of the Female Athlete in Long-Distance Running," reprinted in Kenneth Dyer, *Challenging the Men* (St. Lucia, Queensland: University of Queensland Press, 1982), pp.240-5.

40 Robert Rebar et al., "Editorial: Reproductive Function in Women," *JAMA* 246 (October 2, 1981), p.1590. The editorial was in response to an article by Rose Frisch et al. in the same issue, "Delayed Menarche and Amenorrhea of College Athletes in Relation to Age of Onset of Training," pp.1559-63.

41 See, for example, Margaret Kolka and Lou Stephenson, "The Menstrual Cycle and the Female Athlete," *The Physical Educator* 39 (October 1982), pp.136-41.

42 Robert Malina, in Editor's Corner, *The Physical Educator* 40 (March 1983), pp.51-2; R.M. Malina, "Menarche in Athletes," pp.1-24.

43 An extensive bibliography on this topic is provided in Helen Lenskyj, *Women, Sport and Physical Activity: Research and Bibliography* (Ottawa: Fitness and Amateur Sport, 1986, forthcoming).

44 Mona Shangold, "Sports Gynecology," *The Runner* 3 (June 1981), p.36; see also Shangold, "Sports and Menstrual Function," *Physician and Sportsmedicine* 8 (August 1980), p.68.

45 See, for example, "Diet Link to Runners' Missed Periods," *Self* (October 1983), p.182.

46 See, for example, Andrew Matthews, "Are Periods Necessary?" *Medical News* 14 (November 18, 1982), p.35; Jerilynn Prior and Yvette Vigna, "Reproductive Responses to Endurance Exercises in Women," *Canadian Woman Studies* 4,3 (1983), pp.35-9; Joan Ullyot, *Running Free* (New York: Putnam's, 1981).

Amenorrhea (also termed secondary amenorrhea) refers to the absence of menses for six months; oligomenorrhea refers to intervals of more than 35 days between menses.

47 Colm O'Herlihy, letter to editor, *New England Journal of Medicine* 308 (January 7, 1983), p.50.

48 "Heavy Jogging Hurts Ovulation Doctor Reports," *Toronto Star* January 16, 1982, p.H3.

49 Philip Kingsley, "Hair Loss in Women Tied to Stress of Success," *Toronto Star*, December 26, 1983, p.C3. Kingsley's conclusions were completely impressionistic, legitimated by the observation that "quite a lot" had been written on the subject lately.

50 Alayne Yates et al., "Running — An Analogue of Anorexia?" *New England Journal of Medicine* 308 (February 3, 1983), pp.251-5.

51 Correspondence, *New England Journal of Medicine* 309 (July 7, 1983), pp.47-8.

52 Susan Cushman of the Melpomene Institute quoted by Michael Parrish in "Exercising to the Bone," *Women's Sports* 5 (April 1983), p.32.

53 Halifax doctor quoted by Roma Senn in "Why Everybody's on the Run," *Atlantic Insight* (May 1983), p.22.

CHAPTER THREE

1 Rich, "Compulsory Heterosexuality," pp.631-60; see also Dorothy Kidd, "Getting Physical: Sport and Compulsory Heterosexuality," *Canadian Woman Studies* 4,3 (Spring 1983), pp.62-5.

2 Compare Susan Brownmiller's discussion of femininity as an aesthetic in *Femininity* (New York: Linden/Simon and Shuster, 1984).

3 Some of these class differences were investigated by Eleanor Metheny in *Connotations of Movement in Sport and Dance* (Dubuque, Iowa: Brown, 1965), pp.48-52. For a more recent discussion, in the English context, see Shirley Prendergast, "Stoolball: The Pursuit of Vertigo?" *Women's Studies International Quarterly* 1,1 (1978), pp.15-26.

4 There were, however, the innuendos concerning male homosexual relationships in British public schools.

5 Nellie McClung, *In Times Like These* (1915; Toronto: University of Toronto Press, 1972), pp.86-8.

6 Melville Dent et al., *The Story of the Women Teachers' Association of Toronto* (Toronto: Thomas Nelson and Sons, n.d.), p.19.

7 C.S. Clark, *Of Toronto the Good* (1898; Toronto: Coles, 1970), p.112.

8 "Modern Mannish Maidens," *Blackwood's Magazine* 147 (February 1890, p.259.

9 See, for example, Abba Gould Woolson, ed., *Dress Reform* (1874; New York: Arno Press, 1984); Marion Coe Hawley, "The Freedom of Rational Dress," *Physical Culture* 3 (1900), pp.17-20.

10 Grace Denison, "The Evolution of the Lady Cyclist," *Massey's Magazine* (April 1897), pp.281-4.

11 Christine Herrick, "Women in Athletics: The Athletic Girl not Unfeminine," *Outing* 40 (September 1902), pp.713-21; see also Elizabeth Dryden, "How Athletics May Develop Style in Women," *Outing* 42 (July 1909), pp.413-18.

12 Alice Tweedy, "Homely Gymnastics," *Popular Science Monthly* 40 (February 1892), p.527; see also Martha van Rensselaer, "Chautauqua Reading Course for Housewives: Physical Education Applied to Housework," *The Chautauquan* 34 (February 1902), pp.529-33.

13 Ethel Cartwright, "Athletics and Physical Education," p.281.

14 Benarr MacFadden, "Strong, Beautiful Bodies for Girls and Young Women," *Physical Culture* 3 (May 1900), p.113.

15 See, for example, A.S. Seaholm, "Physical Training," *Athletic Life* 2 (August 1895), p.74; Alex Thompson, "The Necessity of Physical Health in Acquiring an Education," *Canadian Journal of Medicine and Surgery* 17 (June 1905), pp.363-5.

16 See Lillian Faderman, *Surpassing the Love of Men* (New York: William Morrow, 1981), pp.214-30.

17 "Montreal Sport," *Athletic Life* 3 (April 1896), p.231.

18 Clark, *Of Toronto the Good*, p. 112; see also Adelaide Plumptre, "What Shall We Do With 'Our' Flappers?" *MacLean's Magazine* 35 (June 1922), pp.64-5.

19 Definition given by Barbara Fried, "Boys Will Be Boys Will Be Boys: The Language of Sex and Gender," in Ruth Hubbard et al., eds., *Biological Woman* (Cambridge, Massachusetts: Schenkman, 1982), p.47.

20 Douglas Miller of Michigan State University, cited by Thomas Boslooper and Marcia Hayes, *The Femininity Game* (New York: Stein and Day, 1973), pp.92-3.

21 "Modern Mannish Maidens," p.264.

22 Benarr MacFadden, "Womanhood — Muscle," *Physical Culture* 1 (August 1899), pp.181-2.

23 In Toronto, for example, regular women's sport columns appeared in each of the three major newspapers. Women's softball, sponsored by corporations such as the Canadian Pacific Railway and Lakeside Dairy, had a sizeable following throught Ontario. See Helen Lenskyj, "We Want to Play ... We'll Play," *Canadian Woman Studies* 4,3 (1983), pp.15-18.

24 See, for example, Elizabeth Halsey, "The New Sportswoman," *Hygeia* 5 (September 1927), pp.446-8.

25 "Knitted Things for Out-of-Doors," *Chatelaine* 1 (March 1928), p.28; see also Ethel Hoyle, "Dressing the Outdoor Woman," *Outing* 79 (February 1922), pp.225-7; Emma Tucker, "What Two Women Wore," *Outing* 79 (March 1922), p.251.
   The term "fashionalization" is proposed by Ted Polhemus and Lynn Proctor, *Fashion and Anti-Fashion* (London: Thames and Hudson, 1978).

26 See, for example, Fitz, "The Modern Young Person," pp.303-9; Adolphus Knopf, "Tuberculosis among Young Women," *JAMA* 90 (February 1928), pp.532-5. Blanche Johnson made the moral argument in "Our Girls and the Post Bellum," *Woman's Century* (Special Number, 1918), p.77.

27 See, for example, John Cooper, "A Magna Carta for the Girl and Woman in Athletics." pp.21-3, and Blanche Trilling, "Safeguarding Girls' Athletics," pp.8-13 in *Women and Athletics*.

28 Cooper, p.22.

29 W.O. McGeehan, "Glorified Tomboys," *Ladies' Home Journal* 45 (July 1928), pp.25, 72.

30 George Trevor, "Chivalry Aside," *The Outlook* 156 (September 10, 1930), pp.65,79.

31 Women's Section position summarized by Blanche Trilling, "The Playtime of a Million Girls or an Olympic Victory — Which?" in *Women and Athletics*, p.82.

32 Henry Roxborough, "The Illusion of Masculine Supremacy," *Canadian Magazine* 84 (May 1935), p.15. A table of the international amateur athletic records of men and women in comparable events was published in the 1934 World Almanac and reproduced in Catherine Cox Miles, "Sex in Social Psychology," in C.A. Murchison, ed., *Handbook of Social Psychology* (New York: Russell and Russell, 1935), p.774.

CHAPTER FOUR

1 Krafft-Ebing made these kinds of allegations in 1882; see R. von Krafft-Ebing, *Psychopathia Sexualis*, translated by F.G. Rebman (New York: Physicians and Surgeons Books, 1933), pp.398-9.

2 See Lillian Faderman, "The Morbidification of Love Between Women by 19th Century Sexologists," *Journal of Homosexuality* 4,1 (Fall 1978), pp.76-82; Christina Simmons, "Companionate Marriage and the Lesbian Threat," *Frontiers* 4,3 (1979), pp.54-9.

3 See, for example, Floyd Dell, *Love in the Machine Age* (New York: Farrar, 1930); G.V. Hamilton, "The Emotional Life of Modern Woman," in V.F. Calverton and Samuel Schmalhausen, ed., *Women's Coming of Age* (New York: Horace Liveright, 1931), pp.226-9.

4 Phyllis Blanchard, "Sex in the Adolescent Girl," in V.F. Calverton and Samual Schmalhausen, eds., *Sex in Civilization* (New York: Garden City, 1929), pp.558-9.

5 Nan Robins, "I'd Rather Have Beauty Than Brains," *Chatelaine* 4 (February 1931), pp.3, 56-7.

6 Lou Marsh quoted by Frederick Griffin in "Girls, Is Sport Good For You?" *Toronto Star Weekly* (March 31, 1934), p.3; see also Frederick Griffin, "Sport Enhances Womanhood," *Toronto Star Weekly* (October 10, 1931), p.16.

7 Edwin Flemming, "Personality and the Athletic Girl," *School and Society* 39 (February 1934), pp.166-9.

8 Alexandrine Gibb quoted by Griffin in "Girls, is Sport Good For You?"; Griffin, "Sport Enhances Womanhood," p.16.

9 Roxborough, "The Illusion," p.15.

10 Griffin, "Sport Enhances Womanhood," p.16.

11 Ferguson, "Amazon Athletes," pp.9, 32.

12 Roxy Atkins, "An 'Amazon Athlete' Leaps to the Defense of Her Sex," *MacLean's Magazine* 51 (September 15, 1938), p.18. See also Robert Stowell, "Roxy Campbell's Highest Hurdle," *The American Weekly* (January 12, 1947), p.12.

13 Atkins, p.18; "Pretty Girls Set Records at National Swimming Meet," *Life* 7 (August 14, 1939), pp.58-9.

14 "Girls Hit the Line for Appeal," *Toronto Star* (October 19, 1960), p.1.

15 Coverage in the print media ranged from the New York weekly, *Literary Digest* to the small-town Ontario newspaper, *North Bay Nugget*. The major sports in the *Nugget* were basketball and softball, for men's and women's. Gladys Gigg Ross, one of northern Ontario's top all-round athletes, wrote a regular women's sport column, "In the Feminine Realm of Sport," in the 1930s.
   Literary Digest articles of the 1930s included "Eyes of the Tennis World Turn Back to America," vol. 116 (August 5, 1933), p.26; "Fair Golfers Ready for a War on Par," (August 26, 1933), p.25; "Beating a Tradition with Polo-Mallets," vol. 119 (June 15, 1935), p.33; "Modern 'Atalantas' at XI Olympiad," vol. 122 (August 15, 1936), pp.32-4.

16 "Training the Helpless Flapper to Fight Her Own Battles," *The Literary Digest* 94 (August 27, 1927), pp.47-8.

17 Priscilla Leonard, "The Joys of Jiu-Jitsu for Women," *Current Literature* 37 (August 1904), pp.144-5; see also T. Mary Lockyer,

"Jujutsu," *Nature* 75 (January 10, 1907), p.250, for a review of a manual written by an Englishwoman, Mrs. Roger Watts.

18 Photographs which first appeared in *The Sketch* (July 6, 1910), in Midge Mackenzie, *Shoulder to Shoulder* (Harmondsworth, Middlesex: Penguin, 1975), p.255.

19 Ferguson, "Amazon Athletes," p.9; "Modern 'Atalantas'," p.33.

20 See, for example, Geraldine Dare, "Fun in the Open Air," *Everywoman's World* (June 1914), p.11; Norman Raine, "Girls Invade Track and Diamond," *MacLean's Magazine* 38 (August 15, 1925), p.12.

21 "Modern 'Atalantas'," p.33.

22 Interview with Gladys Ross.

23 "Girls' ROTC: New Hampshire Coeds Toughen Up for War," *Life* 14 (January 11, 1943), pp.49-53; For an account of the Canadian Women's Army Corps, see W. Hugh Conrad, *Athene, Goddess of War: CWAC, Their Story* (Dartmouth, N.S.: Writing and Editorial Services, 1983), pp.291-9; see also Susan Hartmann, *The Home Front and Beyond: American Women in the 1940s* (Boston: Twayne, 1982).

24 Major W.E. Fairbairn, "Self-Defense by Women," *New York Times Magazine* (September 27, 1942), pp.22-3.

25 "Ladies of the Little Diamond," *Time* 41 (June 14, 1943), pp.73-4.

26 "Ladies of the Little Diamond"; see also "Old-Timers' Day for Some 'All-American Girls'," *Ms* 11 (October 1982), p.20; W.G. Nicholson, "Women's Pro Baseball Packed the Stands," *WomenSports* (April 1976), pp.23-4.

27 Betty Friedan, *The Feminine Mystique* (New York: Dell, 1963), Chapter One.

28 C.M. Loutitt, "Women: Their Roles and Education," *Journal of Higher Education* 22 (April 1951), pp.202-8, 226.

29 Ben Solomon, "Recreation Problems," *Canadian Welfare* 29 (May 1, 1953), p.5.

30 Joe Trepasso, "The New Look for Women," *Recreation* 42 (February 1949), p.516.

31 "November Yells That Win Games," *The Literary Digest* 83 (November 8, 1924), p.36.

32 *Toronto Star* (November 14, 1942); this and succeeding references are to newspaper clippings in the scrapbooks labelled "1940s" and "1950s," Northern Secondary School Archives, Toronto. Page numbers are missing in some cases.

33 See, for example, *Star* photographs, May 24, 1956, February 15, 1957, in scrapbooks. See also October 7, 1943, August 20, 1953, September 25, 1957; May 22, 1958.

34 In 1959, for example, boys' football, hockey and basketball occupied 17 pages, and girls' activities — basketball, volleyball, badminton, tumbling, swimming, Posture Week, Leaders' Club and Open House — were all contained in 7 pages. A 1959 review of school sport failed to mention any girls' sporting achievements; see Kathy Stephenson and Diane Mitchell, "Past Glories," *NORVOC* (1959), p.18.

35 Halsey, *Women in Physical Education*, pp.47-9.

36 Rita Mae Brown, *Plain Brown Rapper* (Baltimore: Diana Press, 1976), pp.83, 222.

37 Letter to the editor, *WomenSports* 1 (September 1974). p.6.

38 See, for example, Helen Dauncey, "Aids for Your Sports Program for Girls," *Recreation* 46 (November 1952), p.359.

39 Catherine Wilkinson, "Softball Plus ... For Girls," *Recreation* 49 (March 1956), pp.118-19.

40 Northern Technical and Commercial Field Day Program, May 1962, in 1960s scrapbook.

41 "Kemp's Girl Pitcher Strikes Out and Outhits Boy Baseball Players," *Life* 39 (August 22, 1955), pp.51-2.

42 Abby Hoffman's introduction to Jean Cochrane, Abby Hoffman and Pat Kincaid, *Women in Canadian Life: Sports* (Toronto: Fitzhenry and Whiteside, 1977), p.4.

43 "Teenage Olympic Talent," *Life* 32 (June 30, 1952), p.79; see also "Russians Bear Down for Olympics," *Life* 41 (August 6, 1956), pp.91-6.

44 "Rough Creed: There's No Success Without Suffering," *Life* 57 (September 11, 1964), p.42.

45 Keith Moore, "The Sexual Identity of Athletes," *JAMA* 205 (September 9, 1968), pp.163-4; see also "Preserving *la Différence*," *Time* 88 (September 16, 1966), p.72.

46 Moore, p.164; Allen Ryan, "Medical History of the Olympic Games," *JAMA* 205 (September 9, 1968), p.96.

47 Moore, pp.163-4. Moore lists eight other components of sexual phenotype in addition to chromosomal count: external genital, internal reproductive, gonadal, hormonal, genetic, nuclear, psychosexual and socially assigned sex. See also John Money, "Developmental Differences of Femininity and Masculinity Compared," in Seymour Forbes and R. Wilson, eds., *Man and Civilization: The Potential of Women* (New York: McGraw, 1963), pp.55-7.

48 Dyer, *Challenging the Men*, p.66. Dyer predicted dates within next few decades when women's records would equal men's in some athletic events.

49 "Are Girl Athletes Really Girls?" *Life* 61 (October 7, 1966), p.63.

50 Didrikson and Blankers-Koen quoted by Lafayette Smith in "The Girls in the Olympics," *Today's Health* 42 (October 1964), p.30.

51 "Are Girl Athletes," pp.64-5.

52 Unidentified American swimmer quoted by Dyer in *Challenging the Men*, p.66.

53 Prokop quoted in *Sports Illustrated* 44 (October 4, 1971), p.18; see Jan Felshin, "The Dialectic of Woman and Sport," in Ellen Gerber et al., eds. *The American Woman in Sport* (Reading, Massachusetts: Addison-Wesley, 1974), p.204; Dyer, *Challenging the Men*, pp.65-6.

54 Edith McKnight, "The Prevalence of 'Hirsutism' in Young Women," *Lancet* (February 22, 1964), cited by Brownmiller, p.144. It is possible, of course, that Prokop was alluding to "hair on their chests" in a figurative, rather than literal sense, to denote masculinity.

55 Quoted by William Wallace, "Women Are Making Waves in Rowing," *New York Times* (June 17, 1973).

56 Jay Teitel, "Faster, Higher, Stronger," *Toronto Life* (December 1983), p.76; see also "Are Girl Athletes." For a sympathetic story on Walsh,

see "Lessons from Old Olympian: Says Girls Have a Lot to Learn," *Life* 40 (March 19, 1956), pp.113-14.

57 See George Papanicolas and Emil Falk, "General Muscular Hypertrophy Induced by Androgenic Hormone," *Science* 87 (March 11, 1938), pp.238-9; M.T. Lucking, "Steroid Hormones in Sports," *International Journal of Sports Medicine* 3 (1982), pp.65-7.

58 James Wright, "Anabolic Steroids in Athletics," *Exercise and Sport Sciences Reviews* 8 (1980), pp.149-202. See also "It's Not Nice to Fool Mother Nature," *Macleans* 92 (January 8, 1979), p.31, "The Science of Winning," *Macleans* 94 (January 12, 1981), p.38.

59 Moore, "The Sexual Identity," pp.163-4.

60 See Lynda Birke, "From Sin to Sickness: Hormonal Theories of Lesbianism,"in *Biological Woman*, pp.71-90.

61 See Gordon White, "A Woman Swimmer Returns With Medals, Bad Memories," *New York Times* (July 30,1976), p.13; Neil Amdur, "E. German Women's Success Stirs U.S. Rage," (August 1, 1976), p.3. See also Michele Kort, "Is She or Isn't She? Women Athletes and Their Gender Identity," *Chrysalis* 9 (Fall 1979), pp.76-9.

62 Amdur, "E. German Women's Success"; see also Amdur, "U.S. Women Swimmers Win First Gold in Relay, Last Event," *New York Times* (July 26, 1976), p.15.

63 Mary Beth Kelly, Letter to Editor, *New York Times* (August 8, 1976).

64 Connelly quoted in Scorecard, *Sports Illustrated* 51 (November 12, 1979), p.33. On the question of "male hormones," it should be noted that androgen is present in both sexes, as is estrogen, the so-called "female hormone."

65 Decker quoted in "World Championships," *Athletics* (October 1983), p.34.

66 Quoted by James Christie in "Unwomanly Women Sad Reality of Drug Use in Track and Field," *Globe and Mail* (August 13, 1983), p.S3.

67 Lucking, "Steroid Hormones," pp.65-6.

CHAPTER FIVE

1 For a discussion of this research, see M. Ann Hall, *Sport, Sex Roles and Sex Identity* (Ottawa: Canadian Research Institute for the Advancement of Women, 1981), pp.10-17.

2 See Hall, pp.18-22.

3 A. Craig Fisher, "Sports as an Agent of Masculine Orientation," *Physical Educator* 29 (October 1972), p.120.

4 Peter Werner, "The Role of Physical Education in Gender Identification," *Physical Educator* 29 (March 1972), p.28. Werner's list of problems was obviously derived from environmental theories of homosexuality that blamed parental (especially maternal) influences. The list included preference for games of the opposite sex, tolerance of masculinity in girls, mother's reinforcement of passivity in male children, dominant mother and rejecting or absent father.

5 Marjorie Loggia, "On the Playing Fields of History," *Ms* 2 (July 1973), p.63.

6 See, for example, M.T. Saghir and E. Robins, *Male and Female Homosexuality* (Baltimore: Williams-Wilkins, 1973), pp.191-203.

7 John Money and Anke Ehrhardt, *Man & Woman, Boy & Girl* (Baltimore: Johns Hopkins University Press, 1972), p.103.

8 For a critique of Money and Ehrhardt's methodology, see Barbara Fried, "Boys Will Be Boys: The Language of Sex and Gender," in *Biological Woman*, pp.47-69.

9 Saghir and Robins, *Male and Female Homosexuality*, p.201. A 1977 study cited by Sasha G. Lewis, *Sunday's Women* (Boston: Beacon Press, 1979), p.23, reported 82 percent prevalence among lesbians.

10 Janet Hyde et al.,"Tomboyism," *Psychology of Women Quarterly* 2 (Fall 1977), pp.73-5; for anecdotal evidence, see Leanne Schreiber, "Great American Tomboy," *WomenSports* 4 (August, 1977), pp.35-44.

11 "Tomboyism" or "boy-like syndrome" was defined as "polysymptomatic manifestations of preferences and activities that are more usually associated with boys," including "persistent aversions to girls' activities and to girls as playmates" and "a definite preference for the company of boys and boys' activities." (Saghir and Robins, *Male and Female Homosexuality*, p.192). See also Alan Bell, Martin Weinberg and Sue Hammersmith, *Sexual Preference: Its Development in Men and Women* (Indianapolis: Indiana University Press, 1981), p.145.

12 See, for example, Friedan, *The Feminine Mystique*, pp.108-9.

13 Karen Drysdale, "A Socio-Historical Analysis of the Stigmatization of the High Level, Female, Softball Competitor," *Dissertation Abstracts* 39 (1979), p.7221-A.

14 Patsy Neal, *Coaching Methods for Women* (Reading, Massachusetts: Addison-Wesley, 1969), p.105.

15 Quoted by Janice Kaplan, *Women and Sports* (New York: Viking, 1977), pp. 69-72 and Lyn Lemaire, "Women and Athletics: Towards a Physicality Perspective," *Harvard Women's Law Journal* 5 (1982), p.130. See also "Hooping It Up Big in the Corn Belt," *Time* 109 (March 28, 1977), pp.84-5.

16 *More Hurdles to Cross* (Washington: Department of Health, Education and Welfare, 1980), pp.5-6; Kaplan, pp.69-72.

17 "Hooping It Up," p.84; League of Women Voters survey of Iowa high school sport cited by Sheryl Sklorman, "Girl Athletes, Citizen Activists, Title IX: The Three Point Plan," *The High School Journal* 64 (May 1981), p.328. Lemaire, "Women and Athletics," pp.129-31, discusses the legal and philosophical implications of legal cases involving half-court basketball.

18 Paul Hoch, *Rip Off the Big Game* (New York: Doubleday, 1972).

19 Report of the Recreation Committee, *Mayor's Task Force on the Status of Women* (Toronto 1976), pp.104-5.

20 The term is proposed by Philip Goodhart and Chris Chataway, *War Without Weapons* (London: W.H. Allen, 1969). On the question of appropriate fan behaviour and dress, see Jane West and Michael Rich, *A Wife's Guide to Basketball* (New York: Viking Press, 1970).

21 Marty York, "Cheerleaders Not Sazio Fans," *Globe and Mail* (June 2, 1984), p.S7.

22 Pete Axthelm, "The Case of Billie Jean King," *Newsweek* 97 (May 18, 1981), p.133; see also "Facing Up to Billie Jean's Revelations," *Sports Illustrated* 54 (May 11, 1981), pp.13-14; Grace Lichenstein, "Sex and the Female Athlete," *Vogue* 171 (August 1981), p.100; Cheryl McCall, "The Billie Jean King Case: A Friend's Outrage," *Ms* 10 (July 1981), p.100.

23 Unidentified golfer quoted in "The Tour," *Washington Post* (June 12, 1978), p.D8.

24 Axthelm, "The Case," p.133; on the sponsorship issue, see also Wayne Grady, "A Day in the Life: Nancy Lopez," *Weekend Magazine* (July 21, 1979), p.17.

25 "Facing Up," p.13.

26 However, Lichenstein claimed that heterosexual athletes, like most American women, were sufficiently "sophisticated" not to be concerned about lesbianism. See Lichenstein, "Sex and the Female Athlete," p.100.

27 See, for example, Elizabeth Wheeler, "Chris Evert's Toughest Match: Her Struggle to be Mrs. John Lloyd," *Us* (July 10, 1979), pp. 14-15; Richard Lemon, "On the Beach No More, Nancy Lopez and Ray Knight Score a Tie for Golf and Baseball," *People* (April 25, 1983), pp.85-7.

28 William Masters (of the Masters and Johnson team) cited by Gabe Mirkin and Marshall Hoffman, *The Sportsmedicine Book* (Boston: Little, Brown and Co., 1978), p.167; see also "Will Sex Improve Your Game?" *Harper's Bazaar* 113 (May 1980), p.116. An editorial, "Let's Hear It For Women Sports Stars," *Glamour* (September 1983), p.60, cited a recent *Esquire* story and *Glamour's* poll of 100 men to prove that most men were attracted by "an athletic, muscular body."

29 Roy Shephard, *The Fit Athlete* (Oxford: Oxford University Press, 1978), pp.163-5.

30 See, for example, the debate in *Runners' World* 15, 1981: letters to editor on verbal abuse of female runners (January, March and May), p.112; William Dunnett, "The Rape Threat," (June), pp.52-5; letter on "Rape Alert," (August), p.112.

31 Frederick quoted in "Facing Up," p.14.

32 See, for example, Lois Fine, "Personal Best?" *University of Toronto Women's Newsmagazine* 2 (March/April 1982), p.5.

33 Comments on the Canadian Association for the Advancement of Women and Sport are based on my own observations as a member since 1982 and as an executive member, 1984-85, as well as on discussions with founding members.

34 Hoffman quoted by Susan Craig in "Hoffman Blasts Exercise Shows as 'Obscene'," *Sunday Star* (October 2, 1983), p.A5.

35 Quoted by Al Sokol in "Conference to Study Attitude in Women's Sport," *Toronto Star* (September 27, 1983), p.C3.

36 Nora McCabe quoted by Christine Arthurs in "Women's Role in Sport Examined," *Varsity* (October 5, 1983), pp.1, 6.

37 Paula Krebs, "At the Starting Blocks: Women Athletes' New Agenda," *Off Our Backs* 14 (January 1984), pp.2-3.

38 Carol Mann, "Sacrificing a Social Life for Sport," (short version of speech given at the New Agenda conference) *Women's Sports* 6 (February 1984), p.20.

39 Steve Newman, "Making the Right Choice," *Coaching Review* 7 (September/October 1984), p.33. Letters from Bruce Kidd and Lisa Timpf were published in *Coaching Review* 8 (January/February, 1985), p.5.

40 Judith Goldstein, "Women Striving," *Parks and Recreation* 17 (January 1983), pp.78-9.

41 Dorothy Kidd, "Dyke Dynamos," *Pink Ink* (August 1983), pp.14-15.

CHAPTER SIX

1 "Sex Makes a Difference," *Time* 1966, reprinted in *The School Guidance Worker* 23 (December 1967), p.38.

2 Kathleen Collins, "Primary Boys Do Better Alone," *The B.C. Teacher* 45 (February 1966), p.185.

3 Etobicoke Parks and Recreation Commissioner quoted in *Toronto Sun* (July 1977); see M. Ann Hall and Dorothy Richardson, *Fair Ball* (Ottawa: Canadian Advisory Council on the Status of Women, 1982), pp.54-5 for a full discussion of the context.

4 See, for example, Baptist clergyman quoted by Berkeley Rice in "Coming of Age in Sodom and New Milford," *Psychology Today* 9 (September 1975), p.64. In 1974, a U.S. parent complained to the Department of Health, Education and Welfare that body contact between the sexes in mixed physical education classes threatened girls' modesty and was a sign of the "wicked" times. See letter to the Department of Health, Education and Welfare, cited by Patricia Geadelmann, "Physical Education: Stronghold of Sex Role Stereotyping," *Quest* 32,2 (1980), p.196. More recently, the so-called

"Family Protection Act" was introduced in the U.S. congress to limit or prohibit mixed sport; see Hall and Richardson, *Fair Ball*, pp.26-7.

5 See Joan Kutner, "Sex Discrimination in Athletics," *Villanova Law Review* 21 (October 1976), pp.892-4, 898. In the ten-year period up to 1974, when Congress amended the Little League Baseball charter, the integration of girls into the league had been the subject of twenty-two class actions.

6 The first sport-related cases in Canada, which involved girls playing on boys' softball and hockey teams, were brought before provincial human rights commissions in the mid-1970s. For a review of these cases, see Hall and Richardson, pp.18-28, and Helen Lenskyj, *Female Participation in Sport* (Ottawa: Canadian Association for the Advancement of Women and Sport, and Fitness and Amateur Sport, 1984), pp.19-30.

7 John Gardner of the Metro Toronto Hockey League quoted by Ellie Kirzner in "Girls' Hockey Power Play," *Now* (October 25, 1984), p.8.

8 Statement from 1972 *Minnesota Law Review* cited by Florence Grebner, "Sex as a Parameter of Athletic Eligibility," *Physical Educator* 31 (December 1974), p.206.

9 John Sopinka, *Can I Play?* Report of the Task Force on Equal Opportunity in Athletics, Vol. I (September 1983), pp.92-3.

10 See Rosemary Selby, "What's Wrong (and Right) with Coed Physical Education Classes: Secondary School Physical Educators' Views on Title IX Implementation," *Physical Educator* 34 (December 1977), p.189.

11 Wilma Heide, "Feminism for a Sporting Future," in Carole Oglesby, ed., *Women and Sport: From Myth to Reality* (Philadelphia: Lea and Febiger, 1978), pp.195-202.

12 See Sopinka, *Can I Play*, p.94.

13 Sue Palmer, "How Miss San Bernardino Slew the Entire San Diego Basketball Team Without Firing a Single Shot," *WomenSports* 1 (June 1974), p.20.

14 See Geadelmann, "Physical Education," pp.196-9.

15 New York boy quoted by Art Snider in "Boys and Girls Together in Sports?" *Science Digest* 69 (April 1971), p.68.

16 See, for example, Betty Harragan, *Games Your Mother Never Taught You* (New York: Warner Books, 1977), pp.103-16.

17 See Michael Smith, *Violence in Sport* (Toronto: Butterworths, 1983), pp.51-61.

18 In his 1983 review of the literature, Smith found no evidence to confirm or disconfirm his 1972 prediction that female sport was moving towards the male model in terms of violence.

19 See, for example, Freda Adler, *Sisters in Crime* (New York: McGraw-Hill, 1975).

20 See, for example, Sandra Rosenzweig, *Sports Fitness for Women* (New York: Harper and Row, 1982), p.194.

21 Ruth Winter, "Why Women Learn Karate — The Aggressive 'Defense'," *Science Digest* 74 (November 1973), p.21.

22 M. Ann Hall, "Women and the Lawrentian Wrestle," *Canadian Women's Studies* 1,4 (1979), p.39.

23 Photograph, *Toronto Star* (November 23, 1983), p.F5.

24 Ruth Horan, *Judo for Women* (New York: Crown Publishers, 1965), p.6; *Honor Blackman's Book of Self Defence* with Joe and Doug Robinson, (Harmondsworth: Penguin, 1965). For a journalist's account of Horan's approach, see Kevin Brown, "Men Are Full of Weak Points (These Gals Know Where)," *Today's Health* 48 (November 1970, pp.64-6.

25 Iris Young, "Throwing Like a Girl: A Phenomenology of Feminine Body Comportment, Motility and Spatiality," *Human Studies* 3 (April 1980), pp.143-4.

26 Rebecca Moon, "The Karate Underground," *Sportswomen* 1 (September/October 1973), pp.31-3, 36-7. For an example of male instructors' attitudes to women, see "Aikido," *Sports Illustrated* 33 (October 26, 1970), pp.66, 69.

27 Moon, p.32.

28 For the view of attackers as "perverts," see self-defence instructor

quoted by Paul Dalby in "Women Strike Back at Violence," *Toronto Star* (October 17, 1981), p.G1.

29 Karate student quoted by Moon in "The Karate Underground," p.33; see also Diana Gerrity, "Miss Superfist," *Atlantic Monthly* 225 (March 1970), pp.91-3; Linda Pearson, "Learning to be a Survivor: The Liberating Art of Tae Kwondo," *Canadian Women's Studies* 4,1 (1979), pp.49-50.

30 Judo instructor quoted by Winter in "Why Women," p.20.

31 Karate student quoted by Winter, p.20.

32 Duane Valentry, "Don't Be a Crime Victim," *Today's Health* 46 (February 1968), p.22; see also "Working Woman's Guide to Preventing Rape," *Family Circle* (July 17, 1979), p.24. Advice to women on defensive measures appeared regularly in magazines such as *Time, Today's Health* and *Family Circle*.

33 Mary Conroy, *The Rational Woman's Guide to Self-Defense* (New York: Grosset and Dunlop, 1975), p.37. In 1983, the editor of *Women's Sports* published a letter from an elderly woman who stated that young women running in shorts were responsible for the rising incidence of rape. See Dorothy Browning's letter, *Women's Sports* 5 (December 1983) p.9 and Helen Lenskyj's letter in response, *Women's Sports* 6 (June 1984), p.10.

34 "The City: In Defense of Women," *Time* 87 (April 15, 1966), p.71; see also Margaret Morrison, "They Graduate as Tigers," *Parks and Recreation* 3 (June 1968), pp.26-8, 57-8, and Victoria Pellegrino, "What a Scream Can Do For You," *Today's Health* 51 (June 1973), pp.29-33, 64-8; "Public Safety: How Can a Girl Defend Herself?" *Time* 89 (February 10, 1967), p.43.

35 See, for example, Pauline Bart, "A Study of Women Who Both Were Raped and Avoided Rape," *Journal of Social Issues* 37, 4 (1981), pp.123-37. Inadvertently perpetuating the victim-blaming approach was a 1981 psychology article that identified victims' non-verbal cues, so that individuals might avoid appearing vulnerable to attack. See Betty Grayson and Morris Stein, "Attracting Assault: Victims' Nonverbal Cues," *Journal of Communication* 31,1 (1981), pp.68-75.

36 V.D. Seefeldt et al., "Scope of Youth Sports Programs in the State of Michigan," in F. Smoll and R. Smith, eds., *Psychological Perspectives in Youth Sports* (Washington: Hemisphere, 1978), pp.50-2.

37 Bruce Kidd et al., *For Amateur Boxing*, The Report of the Ontario Amateur Boxing Review Committee (Toronto: Ministry of Tourism and Recreation, 1983), pp.112-13.

38 Quoted by Al Sokol in "Boxer Hotchkiss Takes the First Round," *Toronto Star* (November 22, 1983), p.F6.

39 Clyde Gray quoted by Rick Fraser in "This Champion Keeps Punching for Women's Boxing in Ontario," *Toronto Star* (December 26, 1981), p.D6.

40 Hotchkiss quoted by Sokol in "Boxer Hotchkiss," p.F6. The possibility of blows to the breast was just as high in some martial arts, and manufacturers of protective equipment for these sports developed women's chest protectors that could withstand the impact of a punch or kick.

41 Sopinka, *Can I Play*, Appendix 6, pp.4-5.

42 See, for example, "Female Athletes Need Good Bras, MD Reports," *Physician and Sportsmedicine* 5 (August 1977), p.15; Gale Gehlsen and Marge Albohm, "Evaluation of Sports Bras," *Physician and Sportsmedicine* 8 (October 1980), pp.89-97.

43 The author of a 1979 article on traumatic breast cancer claimed that it was "axiomatic that medicine and law often adhere to different standards of proof in determining the cause of an injury." See Michael Stevens, "Traumatic Breast Cancer," *Medical Trial Technique Quarterly* 25 (Summer 1979), p.6; see also Nathan Flaxman, "Breast Cancer," *Medical Trial Technique Annual* (1967), pp.73-4.

44 In a 1978 sex discrimination case at the University of Toronto, the Ombudsman ruled that the question was not whether the risk to women in mixed soccer was greater, but rather whether the risk was *unacceptably high.* See Kidd, *For Amateur Boxing*, p.41. Similarly, some American courts have ruled "protection from unreasonable risk" unconstitutional. See *More Hurdles to Cross*, p.8, note 13.

45 Geadelmann, "Physical Education," p.196; Marjorie Blaufarb, "As I See Coed Physical Education," *Today's Education* 67 (April/May 1978), pp.64-6.

46 Christine Sauveur quoted by Peter McCusker, "In This Corner, Christine Rising Amateur Wrestler," *Toronto Star* (December 5, 1979), p.A26.

47 Robert Clark quoted by Bob McKenzie in "Wrestling for Women?" *Upstream* (January 1979), p.16; Clark's "Guidelines for Establishing the Physical Fitness Levels of the Girls and Women," typescript, n.d. [1982].

48 Kidd, *For Amateur Boxing*, pp.24-5, 111-12, and personal communication during the research stage of the report, 1982-83.

49 Mary Duquin, "Reflections on Sexual Segregation in Youth Sport," *The Physical Educator* 38 (May 1981), p.67.

50 Mary Duquin, "The Importance of Sport in Building Women's Potential," *JOPERD* 53 (March 1982), p.20. Duquin agreed, however, that current levels of violence against women warranted girls' and women's participation in appropriate contact sports.

CHAPTER SEVEN

1 Kenneth Cooper, *Aerobics* (New York: Bantam Books, 1968).

2 President's Council ad in *Good Housekeeping* 180 (February 1975), p.25.

3 Richard Corliss, "The New Ideal of Beauty," *Time* 120 (August 30, 1982), p.40. See also Paul Howard and John MacKay, "Singing the Body Eclectic," *Toronto Life Fashion* (Summer 1982), p.58.

4 See Ahmed Belkaoui and Janice Belkaoui, "A Comparative Analysis of the Roles Portrayed by Women in Print Advertisements: 1958, 1970, 1972," *Journal of Marketing Research* 13 (May 1976), p.171; Alison Poe, "Active Women in Ads," *Journal of Communication* 26 (Autumn 1976), pp.185-92.

5 Le Sport ads, *Harper's Bazaar* 112 (September 1979), p.14; *Cosmopolitan* (June 1979), pp.22-3.

6 See Stayfree ads in *Good Housekeeping, Glamour, Cosmo, Redbook*, 1977-83.

7 See, for example, Kidd, "Getting Physical," pp.62-3; Jacqui Salmon, "Cutting Class," *Women's Sports* 5 (March 1983), p.60.

8 "The National Leotard League," *Sports Illustrated* 59 (November 18,1983), p.30; advertising package distributed by Inwood & Associates, Toronto, August 14, 1984. See also Helen Lenskyj, "Sexercise Sells," *Mudpie* 5 (December 1984), p.17.

9 See, for example, Laura Grengo-De Rosa, "Aerobic Awareness," *WomenSports* 4 (December 1982), p.23; Leigh Fenly, "Dance Exercise Guidelines Planned," *Physician and Sportsmedicine* 12 (September 1984), pp.31-2. For another perspective, see "Blood, Sweat and Beers," *Toronto Life* (March 1984), p.45.

10 Corliss, "The New Ideal," p.44.

11 J.D. Reed, "America Shapes Up," *Time* 118 (November 2, 1981), p.75.

12 *Karen Kain's Fitness Book* as told to Marilyn Linton (Toronto: Doubleday, 1983); Gayle Olinekova, *Go For It* (New York: Simon and Schuster, 1982). For more of this genre, see, for example, *Jane Fonda's Workout Book* (New York: Simon and Schuster, 1982).

13 See Helen Lenskyj, "Expo Catcher, Gary Carter, in Bikini?" *Mudpie* 3 (June 1983), p.18.

14 Abby Hoffman's columns in "Health Centre," *Chatelaine*, 1980-82. Of the articles on fitness listed in *Readers' Guide to Periodicals* (March 1979 - February 1980), 66 percent were published in eleven women's fashion magazines. See, for example, "Getting in the Swim (with a Sensational Shape)," *Cosmopolitan* (June 1979), pp.284-7.

15 A 1984 *Toronto Sun* ad for half-price fitness club membership showed a woman wearing only a bikini bottom, observed by an admiring man. The caption read, "Get twice the looks at half the price." Superfitness Centres ad, *Toronto Sun* (August 13, 1984), p.7. See also Gold's ad, *Toronto Sun* (May 7, 1984), p.16.

16 Champions Centres ad, advertising section, *Star TV Week* (March 3, 1984), p.H6. Further examples of the leotarded figure in advertising include a Boxing Day sale ad illustrated by a woman wearing boxing gloves and a leotard, in the same seductive pose as women in fitness ads; similarly, an ad for a topless dancing cabaret had the same leotarded figure in much the same pose. See, for example, Stitches ad, *Toronto Star* (December 26, 1983), p.A9; *Toronto Sun*, passim.

17 "A Feminist Health and Fitness Counselling Centre," presentation by Lorraine Greaves and Deborah Barr, CAAW&S Conference, Katimavik, Quebec, May 1984. See also Janet Camilleri, "Fitness First," *Toronto Life Fashion* (Spring 1984), pp.17-20; "Hefty Woman's Big on Fitness," *Toronto Star* (October 15, 1983), p.3.

18 Quoted by Howard and MacKay in "Body Eclectic," p.62.

19 Some criticism's of female bodybuilders' muscularity, however, were based on suspicions of anabolic steroid use. See Jack Horn, "A Dangerous Edge," *Psychology Today* 17 (November 1983), p.68; Patty Freedson et al., "Physique, Body Composition, and Psychological Characteristics of Competitive Female Body Builders," *Physician and Sportsmedicine* 11 (May 1983), pp.85-90.

20 Patricia Malloy quoted by Howard and MacKay in "Body Eclectic," p.62.

21 Lynne Pirie quoted by Trent Frayne in "Aiming at Equal Muscles," *Globe and Mail* (March 30, 1984), p.S1. See also "She Proves Muscles Can Be Sexy," *Toronto Star* (January 26, 1984), p.D1.

22 Fern Schumer, "Life, Liberty and the Pursuit of Muscle Power," *Forbes* 123 (May 28, 1979), p.35.

23 Jan Otteson, "Weight Lifting: Don't Put It Down," *Cosmopolitan* 194 (April 1983), p.136. See also Trixie Rosen, *Strong and Sexy: The New Body Beautiful* (New York: Delilah, 1983).

24 Mary Sheppard, "Pumping Iron and Dreaming of '10'," *Maclean's* 93 (July 14, 1980), p.36.

25 Marta Tarbell, "$25,000 Curves: How Women are Chiseling Them out of Female Muscle," *Self* (October 1983), pp.170. See "Pumping Iron, Chapter II," *Time* 114 (November 12, 1979), p.131.

26 Snyder quoted by Charles Gaines in "Iron Sisters," *Psychology Today* 17 (November 1983), p.66.

27 Barrilleaux quoted by Horn in "A Dangerous Edge," p.68.

28 Gaines, "Iron Sisters," p.69.

29 Sheppard, "Pumping Iron," p.36. Three years later, the winner of the Women's World Bodybuilding Championship, Carla Dunlap, was not a woman with a typically feminine physique. As a black woman, too, her success was especially noteworthy.

30 Dudley Sargent, "Are Athletics Making Girls Masculine?" *Ladies' Home Journal* 29 (March 1912), pp.11, 71-2.

SELECTED BIBLIOGRAPHY

Boslooper, Thomas and Marcia Hayes. *The Femininity Game*. New York: Stein and Day, 1974.

Cochrane, Jean, Abby Hoffman and Pat Kincaid. *Women in Canadian Life: Sports*. Toronto: Fitzhenry and Whiteside, 1977.

Duquin, Mary. "Reflections on Sexual Segregation in Youth Sport." *The Physical Educator* 38 (1981): 65-70.

Dyer, Kenneth. *Challenging the Men*. St. Lucia, Queensland: University of Queensland Press, 1982.

Ehrenreich, Barbara and Deidre English. *For Her Own Good: 150 Years of the Experts' Advice to Women*. Garden City, New York: Anchor Books, 1979.

Faderman, Lillian. *Surpassing the Love of Men*. New York: William Morrow, 1981.

Felshin, Jan. "The Dialectic of Women and Sport." In *The American Woman in Sport*, edited by Ellen Gerber et al., pp. 179-279. Reading, Massachusetts: Addison-Wesley, 1974.

Fried, Barbara. "Boys Will Be Boys Will Be Boys: The Language of Sex and Gender." In *Biological Woman*, edited by Ruth Hubbard et al., pp.47-69. Cambridge, Massachusetts: Schenkman, 1982.

Geadelmann, Patricia. "Physical Education: Stronghold of Sex Role Stereotyping." *Quest* 32 (1980): 192-200.

Goldstein, Judith. "Women Striving." *Parks and Recreation* 17,1 (1983): 70-81.

Gurney, Helen. *Girls' Sport: A Century of Progress*. Don Mills, Ontario: Ontario Federation of School Athletic Associations, 1979.

Hall, M. Ann. "Women and the Lawrentian Wrestle." *Canadian Women's Studies* 1,4 (1979): 39-41.

Hall, M. Ann. *Sport, Sex Roles and Sex Identity*. Ottawa: Canadian Research Institute for the Advancement of Women, 1981.

Hall, M. Ann and Dorothy Richardson. *Fair Ball*. Ottawa: Canadian Advisory Council on the Status of Women, 1982.

Harragan. Betty. *Games Your Mother Never Taught You*. New York: Warner, 1978.

Heide, Wilma. "Feminism for a Sporting Future." In *Women and Sport: From Myth to Reality*, edited by Carole Oglesby, pp.195-202. Philadelphia: Lea and Febiger, 1978.

Hyde, Janet et al. "Tomboyism." *Psychology of Women Quarterly* 2 (1977): 73-5.

Kaplan, Janice. *Women and Sports*. New York: Viking, 1977.

Kidd, Dorothy. "Getting Physical: Compulsory Heterosexuality and Sport." *Canadian Woman Studies* 4,3 (1983): 62-5.

Krebs, Paula. "At the Starting Blocks: Women Athletes' New Agenda." *Off Our Backs* 14,1 (1984): 2-3.

Lenskyj, Helen. *Female Participation in Sport*. Ottawa: Canadian Association for the Advancement of Women and Sport, and Fitness and Amateur Sport, 1984.

Lenskyj, Helen. *Women, Sport and Physical Activity: Research and Bibliography*. Ottawa: Fitness and Amateur Sport, 1986, forthcoming.

Loggia, Marjorie. "On the Playing Fields of History." *Ms* July 1973, pp.63-4.

MacKinnon, Catherine. "Feminism, Marxism, Method, and the State: An Agenda for Theory." *Signs* 7 (1982): 515-44.

Malina. Robert. "Menarche in Athletes: A Synthesis and Hypothesis." *Annals of Human Biology* 10 (1983): 1-24.

Metheny, Eleanor. *Connotations of Movement in Sport and Dance*. Dubuque, Iowa: Brown, 1963.

Pearson, Linda. "Learning to be a Survivor: The Liberating Art of Tae Kwondo." *Canadian Women's Studies* 4,1 (1979): 49-50.

Poe, Alison. "Active Women in Ads," *Journal of Communication* 26,4 (1976): 185-92.

Prendergast, Shirley. "Stoolball: The Pursuit of Vertigo?" *Women's Studies International Quarterly* 1,1 (1978): 15-26.

Prior, Jerilynn and Yvette Vigna. "Reproductive Responses to Endurance Exercises in Women." *Canadian Woman Studies* 4,3 (1983): 35-9.

Rich, Adrienne. "Compulsory Heterosexuality and Lesbian Existence." *Signs* 5 (1980): 631-60.

Roberts, Wayne. "'Rocking the Cradle for the World': The New Woman and Maternal Feminism, Toronto, 1877-1914." In *A Not Unreasonable Claim*, edited by Linda Kealey, pp.15-46. Toronto: Women's Press, 1979.

Simmons, Christina. "Companionate Marriage and the Lesbian Threat." *Frontiers* 4,3 (1979): 54-9.

Sklorman, Sheryl. "Girl Athletes, Citizen Activists, Title IX: The Three Point Plan." *The High School Journal* 64 (1981): 326-30.

Ullyot, Joan. *Running Free*. New York: Putnam's, 1981.

Vertinsky, Patricia. "The Effect of Changing Attitudes Toward Sexual Morality upon the Promotion of Physical Education for Women in 19th Century America." *Canadian Journal of History of Sport and Physical Education* 7,2 (1976): 26-38.

Willis, Paul. "Women in Sport in Ideology." In *Sport, Culture and Ideology*, edited by Jennifer Hargreaves, pp.117-35. London: Routledge Kegan Paul, 1982.

Young, Iris. "Throwing Like a Girl: A Phenomenology of Feminine Body Comportment, Motility and Spatiality." *Human Studies* 3 (1980): 137-56.